THEODORE DRANGE

Type
Crossings

MOUTON & CO.

TYPE CROSSINGS

JANUA LINGUARUM

STUDIA MEMORIAE
NICOLAI VAN WIJK DEDICATA

edenda curat

C. H. VAN SCHOONEVELD

INDIANA UNIVERSITY

SERIES MINOR

NR. XLIV

1966

MOUTON & CO.

THE HAGUE · PARIS

TYPE CROSSINGS

SENTENTIAL MEANINGLESSNESS
IN THE BORDER AREA OF
LINGUISTICS AND PHILOSOPHY

by

THEODORE DRANGE

IDAHO STATE UNIVERSITY

1966
MOUTON & CO.
THE HAGUE · PARIS

Printed in The Netherlands.

PREFACE

The problem posed in this book is: what makes sentences like "the theory of relativity is blue" meaningless? I claim that this is a very profound and complex problem. However, no book or article has ever been aimed exclusively at it. In both philosophical and linguistic circles, its true complexity has gone largely unrecognized. The reason for this is that everyone thinks he has a ready solution: sentences like "the theory of relativity is blue" are meaningless because they violate conventions of language. There may be some debate as to whether these conventions are definitional or grammatical or some third sort, but that the solution lies in the appeal to language has gone completely unquestioned. Part of my purpose in the present book is to question this assumption, and, in fact, to refute it. This is the part that I feel I have most successfully accomplished. The other part, that of putting forward an alternative solution, is not brought off quite as well, despite the fact that most of the book is put into its service.

My method, throughout, is theoretical, rather than experimental or descriptive. My assumptions are, for the most part, a priori rather than empirical. And my style is dialectical rather than expository. The whole book is a kind of running debate between advocates of different philosophical and linguistic outlooks. For every stand I take, I try to anticipate the critic's reply and defend my position against that reply. Whether or not I have succeeded in every case must be left to the future to decide.

The reader needs to be warned of two terminological peculiarities of the book. First, although I use the word 'type' throughout, the word 'category' would probably be more appropriate, for I do not attribute to the word 'type' the technical sense given to it in Russell's Theory of Types. Part of the explanation for my use of the word 'type' is that Arthur Pap used it in his paper "Types and Meaninglessness", and it was my response to that paper that provided the initial spark for the present work. But my main motive in using 'type' instead of 'category' is that it is a shorter word, and furthermore, expressions containing it (e.g., 'type of thing', 'type of activity', 'type of property', 'type crossing') are less awkward than the corresponding expressions substituting 'category' for 'type'.

The second terminological peculiarity is that I apply the adjectives 'true' and 'false' to *sentences* (as well as to propositions). Some philosophers would object to this, saying that sentences are not the type of thing that could be true or false, that only propositions (i.e., what sentences express) can be said to be true or false. But I have never seen any good argument for this view. On the contrary, Alfred Tarski has provided us with the following model: the sentence "snow is white" is true if and only if snow is white. To this, we may add: the sentence "snow is white" is false if and only if snow is not white. I find these pronouncements quite unobjectionable. And they indicate with maximum economy what is meant by saying of a certain *sentence* ("snow is white") that it is true or that it is false. At any rate, my application of truth and falsity to sentences may be interpreted in terms of this model. If the reader is still inclined to balk, then I suggest he regard the application of truth and falsity to sentences as only a space-saving device. If necessary, any application of truth or falsity to a sentence could be translated into an application of truth or falsity to a proposition, in accordance with the following model: the sentence "snow is white" is true (or false) if and only if the proposition expressed by it is true (or false). Once this is understood, there should not be any further objection.

An earlier and briefer version of this book constituted my dissertation for the Ph. D. degree in philosophy which was received from Cornell University in June 1963. I would like to acknowledge my great indebtedness to the following philosophers for their comments and criticisms directed at that earlier work: Max Black, Charles Parsons, Zeno Vendler, Walter Cerf, and Keith Donnellan. Many of the objections against which I defend my claims are objections originally expressed by one or more of these philosophers. Finally, the philosopher whose publications have inspired me to the greatest extent is my former teacher, the late Arthur Pap. It is my greatest regret that he died before an exchange of ideas between us on the topic of type crossings was possible.

May 17, 1965   THEODORE DRANGE

TABLE OF CONTENTS

INTRODUCTION

Philosophers have attempted to support their belief in the existence of meaningless sentences by formulating examples such as the following:

(1) The theory of relativity is blue.
(2) The number 5 weighs more than the number 6.
(3) Socrates is a prime number.
(4) Quadruplicity drinks procrastination.
(5) Smells are loud.
(6) I have eaten a loud clap.
(7) Moral perfection is a prime number.
(8) Chemistry is a greater ordinal than the concept of truth.

There is an inclination to say of these and similar sentences that if *any* sentences are meaningless, *they* are. This inclination does not exist for various other kinds of sentences which have been called "meaningless" by philosophers, such as self-referential sentences, analytic sentences whether true or false, sentences which express value judgments or religious or metaphysical ideas. These are rarely cited as clear cases of meaningless sentence because there is wide disagreement as to whether or not they are meaningless. On the other hand, sentences such as (1)–(8) are often given as clear examples of meaningless sentence. This may be their only use.

It might be objected that sentences (1)–(8) are not meaningless after all, because interpretations can be given to them which would render them not only intelligible, but true. For example, consider sentence (1) in connection with the following context:

An Air Force secretary is ordered to distribute copies of a training manual concerned with the theory of relativity, and asks, "How am I to tell it from the manual on martini mixing?" The reply: "The theory of relativity is blue; martini mixing is light green."

Similarly, sentence (2) could be uttered in a printing shop by a type setter. Sentence (3) could have reference to a numbered list of philosophers' names. Sentence (4) could be a poetical way of saying that having the concept of quadruplicity requires much procrastination. And the others could also be given interpretations in an analogous way. These interpretations may be unusual, but they are not unreasonable. Hence, sentences (1)–(8) should not be considered meaningless.

To avoid this objection, we must understand that sentences (1)–(8) are to be interpreted literally, without any of their terms being taken in an unusual way. When they are thus interpreted, most people would consider sentences (1)–(8) to be meaningless. Also, it must be understood that the expression "sentences such as (1)–(8)" is to refer only to sentences which are in a similar way to be interpreted literally. It would then be quite plausible to say that all sentences such as (1)–(8) are meaningless and to use them as examples of meaningless sentence.

Some writers on the subject prefer to speak of sentences such as (1)–(8) as *odd* rather than meaningless. I have no quarrel with this terminology. But it should be realized that what makes them odd is the fact that, unlike ordinary sentences, sentences such as (1) –(8) need to be given some *special* interpretation in order to be understood. If they are interpreted in a literal and straightforward way, then they are unintelligible. The problem comes in at this point: just *why* are they unintelligible when taken literally? It is towards a solution to this philosophical problem that the present book is directed.

A person who utters a sentence such as (1)–(8) seems to be saying of one type of thing something that has application only to another type of thing. For example, in sentence (1), something is said of the theory of relativity (namely, that it is blue) which has application only to a different type of thing (viz.

things which have spatial extension). For this reason, there is point in calling such sentences as (1)–(8) by the name "type crossings". They involve a crossing of types or type boundaries. At any rate, let the term 'type crossing' be understood, for the time being, as referring to sentences which are like (1)–(8) in the specified way.

All type crossings, then, are meaningless, and this is so by virtue of the interpretation given to them. It is of the utmost importance to understand that what makes a sentence a type crossing is the interpretation given to it, which is not necessarily its prima-facie meaning. For example, consider the sentence:

(9) That mechanism has two springs in it.

Sentence (9) would normally be taken to be a perfectly meaningful sentence of English. But suppose the word 'spring', which appears in it, were understood to mean 'the first season of the year'. Then (9) would be a type crossing, being equivalent to "that mechanism has two first seasons in it". From this it can be seen that whether or not a sequence of words is a type crossing is (sometimes at least) a matter of how certain specific words in it are to be interpreted.

Consider a slightly different example:

(10) Necessity is the mother of invention.

This sentence is normally understood to be a metaphor. As such it is quite meaningful and not a type crossing. Some people might hold (10) to be true, while others might feel that something other than necessity is the mother of invention. But suppose (10) were understood literally. That is, suppose the expression 'is the mother of' were interpreted in exactly the same way as in "Mary is the mother of John", where the giving birth, the period of gestation, etc. are all understood. Then it seems that (10) would be a type crossing. Thus, again, whether or not a sequence is a type crossing is strictly a matter of interpretation; what distinguishes a metaphorical sentence from a type crossing composed of the same words in the same order is the meaning or interpretation to be given to some of the words. No doubt most metaphorical sentences would be type crossings if they were taken literally.

It is important to see that what determines how a word is to be interpreted is the actual meaning given to it in the context in which it appears. Its interpretation is not determined by either its origin or most usual meaning. One writer who seems to have overlooked this point is R. C. Cross. He says the following:

> One should not expect that in their behaviour words will always fall into sharp and clearly defined exclusive patterns. A crossing of patterns may not always produce nonsense – as a trivial example, while we might want for most purposes to distinguish the logical patterns of colour words and sound words, a phrase like "loud colour" makes good sense; and some collocations of this sort can be highly striking and illuminating.[1]

What I object to is reference to the expression 'loud colour' as "a crossing of patterns" and reference to the term 'loud', as it appears in that expression, as a "sound word". In the *American College Dictionary*, the seventh meaning given to 'loud' is "excessively striking to the eye, or offensively showy, as colors, dress or the wearer, etc." Given this interpretation, 'loud' is *not* a sound word, and 'loud colour' does not involve any "crossing of patterns", at least not in anything like the sense in which type crossings do. There may be a crossing of patterns with respect to the origins or usual meanings of the words 'loud' and 'colour', which is apparently what Cross intends to say, but there is none with respect to the way the words are *actually* interpreted in this context. And it is only in the latter sense that type crossings involve a "crossing of patterns". Hence, insofar as it is correct, Cross's remark that "a crossing of patterns may not always produce nonsense" does not entail that type crossings are sometimes meaningful.

By this discussion, I hope to have shown why type crossings must be regarded as meaningless rather than as metaphorically true. But now let us consider the quite different objection that

---

[1] R. C. Cross, "Category Differences", *Proceedings of the Aristotelian Society*, LIX (1959), p. 270.

type crossings are not meaningless, but simply *false*. For example, with respect to the sentence "the theory of relativity is blue", it might be argued that since the theory of relativity is not the type of thing that can have a color, obviously it cannot be blue. Therefore, any sentence asserting that it is blue must be a false sentence. Hence, type crossings such as "the theory of relativity is blue" are not meaningless, but simply false.

To this view, Arthur Pap has the following reply:

If a theory of meaning goes to such extremes of tolerance as to condemn no sentences whatever as meaningless, it does not deserve serious consideration. Such is, for example, the theory that any sentence is meaningful provided it conforms to the rules of syntax. For the rules of syntax presumably *define* what strings of words are to be called "sentences", hence a pattern of words that fails to conform to those rules is not so much a meaningless sentence as no sentence at all. Those who seriously adhere to this theory, if there are any, would then have to say that the sentence "quadratic equations like coffee" is meaningful, though undoubtedly *false*. But if they thus refuse to admit that some sentences are not so much false as meaningless, they will simply have to draw a distinction between *two kinds of falsehood* which turns out to differ very little from the explicitly repudiated distinction between meaningful and meaningless sentences. For surely the sentence "quadratic equations like coffee" is not false in quite the same sense as "quadratic equations contain only one constant" or "all Englishmen like coffee better than tea" is false. Corresponding to any predicate there is a range of significance which, as we have seen, must be distinguished from the truth-range which it comprises. Whether such significance ranges can be precisely delimited and how, is, indeed, a difficult question. Yet, rough outlines are always possible and cannot raise any serious doubt. Only entities endowed with organs of taste, for example, could significantly be said to like coffee, and only symbolic formulae could significantly be said to contain constants. Thus, some such distinction as between semantically incorrect and factually incorrect predications would have to be acknowledged anyway.[2]

Pap's objection to the view that type crossings are false rather than meaningless turns on the fact that there is a difference

---

[2] Arthur Pap, *Elements of Analytic Philosophy* (New York, The Macmillan Company, 1949), pp. 322-323.

between ordinary false sentences, such as "Englishmen like coffee better than tea", and type crossings, such as "quadratic equations like coffee better than tea". But what, exactly, is the nature of this difference? Perhaps it is not as clear-cut as Pap makes it out to be. Consider, for example, the following series of sentences:

(a) Englishmen like coffee better than tea.
(b) Squirrels like coffee better than tea.
(c) Protozoa like coffee better than tea.
(d) Bacteria like coffee better than tea.
(e) Milkweed plants like coffee better than tea.
(f) Stones like coffee better than tea.
(g) Electrons like coffee better than tea.
(h) Quadratic equations like coffee better than tea.

Pap would draw a sharp distinction between the sense in which (a) would be called false and the sense in which (h) might be called false. But perhaps this difference is not so much a difference in kind as a difference in degree.[3] Sentences (a)–(h) seem to be arranged in a graded series in such a way that it is not at all clear where a line is to be drawn to distinguish the "factually incorrect" sentences from the "semantically incorrect" sentences (or the false from the meaningless).[4]

---

[3] To put it very roughly, two things differ in kind when one has a property which the other lacks, and they differ in degree when there is a property which one possesses to a greater degree than the other. For example, a full-grown elephant and a baby elephant differ *in degree* with respect to size and also age. However, an elephant is different *in kind* from any other species of animal, such as, say, a giraffe, for each has many properties which the other lacks altogether.

[4] Some other examples of graded series having this quality are the following:

Grass is blue.
The United States is blue.
An electron is blue.
A high pitched sound is blue.
The theory of relativity is blue.
  Lassie drinks whiskey.
  Bacteria drink dust.

Socrates is a Roman.
Socrates is a caveman.
Socrates is a wasp.
Socrates is a milkweed plant.
Socrates is a prime number.

In what way might there be a difference in degree between (a) and (h)? Perhaps it might be said that Englishmen have *more in common* with things which like coffee better than tea than do quadratic equations. There are many properties which Englishmen share with things which like coffee better than tea that are not possessed by quadratic equations, such as being a physical object, being alive, having organs of taste, and so on. On the other hand, there are very few properties which quadratic equations share with things which like coffee better than tea,[5] and it seems that Englishmen have all of them also. It is in this sense that the difference between (a) and (h) might be said to be one of degree.

However, there is at least one technical difficulty with this notion of a difference in degree. It might be argued that the number of properties shared by quadratic equations and things which like coffee better than tea is actually infinite. For example, there are the following properties:

the property of not being composed of exactly one stone
the property of not being composed of exactly two stones
the property of not being composed of exactly three stones
etc.[6]

Since there are an infinite number of such properties, it seems that we cannot say that Englishmen have more properties in common with things which like coffee better than tea than do quadratic equations. In fact, according to this argument, the number of properties shared by any two things is infinite. This

---

Milkweed plants drink stones.
Electrons drink sunbeams.
Quadruplicity drinks procrastination.

[5] The only ones I can think of are such properties as being something which a sentence might be about, being of interest to someone, being talked and thought about, and so on.
[6] In addition, there are disjunctive properties, such as the following:
being of interest to someone or composed of exactly one stone
being of interest to someone or composed of exactly two stones
being of interest to someone or composed of exactly three stones
and so on to infinity.

would certainly destroy the notion of a difference in degree, as suggested above.

Because of such technical difficulties, it is questionable whether the notion of a difference in degree between type crossings and ordinary false sentences could be given an adequate precise definition. But even if it could be given such a definition, the more important question would remain: is the difference between type crossings and ordinary false sentences *only* one of degree or is there also a difference in kind? Clearly, what Pap needs for his argument is a difference in kind. And one of my main purposes will be to show that there *is* such a difference and to expound in detail what it is. This task will be closely bound up with that of explaining what type crossings are, or stating the necessary and sufficient conditions for being a type crossing. But quite aside from this matter, it is clear that I have not as yet settled the original issue. Given that there *is* a difference in kind between type crossings and ordinary false sentences, does this difference need to be characterized in terms of falsity versus meaninglessness, or can it be properly characterized in terms of two kinds of falsity? This is no minor terminological issue. It will be shown in Chapter 3 that much turns on it. Bearing this in mind, one of the conclusions I shall attempt to establish in Chapter 2 is that the characterization in terms of two kinds of falsity is quite legitimate after all.

A PRIORI FALSITY

2.1. THE NEGATIONS OF TYPE CROSSINGS

Before discussing the question of the difference in kind between type crossings and ordinary false sentences, I shall first attempt to establish that type crossings *can* legitimately be characterized as false sentences. This would follow, I believe, from the proposition that the negations of type crossings are true. And this latter point has been quite ably defended by two philosophers, A. C. Ewing and A. N. Prior.

Ewing says the following:

It is usually held that a sentence which ascribes to something a relatively determinate value of a determinable which does not qualify it is meaningless, whether the determinate value is asserted or denied of it. The most usual example of this cited lately at Cambridge is –quadratic equations go to race-meetings–, the example in my days at Oxford was –virtue is a fire-shovel–. It is generally held that such statements are not false but meaningless. It is further held that their contradictories, –quadratic equations do not go to race meetings– and –virtue is not a fire-shovel–, are not true, but likewise meaningless. This, however, I am prepared to dispute. For after all, –quadratic equations do not go to race-meetings– is entailed by –quadratic equations do not move in space– and entails –quadratic equations do not watch the Newmarket horse-races–; but, if it is capable of entailing and being entailed, surely it must be a proposition and not a mere meaningless set of words.[1]

Prior says the following:

My proof that virtue is not square is a simple syllogism – what is square has some shape, but virtue has no shape, therefore virtue is not square. That my left eye is not square would of course have to

<hr>

[1] A. C. Ewing, "Meaninglessness", *Mind*, XLVI (1937), p. 360.

be proved a little differently; the point about my left eye is not that it has no shape but that it has *another* shape. But this difference in the character of the proofs that one would give for the two statements – and from a logical point of view the difference is not very great (it is only that between the mood Camestres and the mood Cesare) – this difference whether great or small, is *only* a difference in the proofs one gives; it does not mean or entail that when I say that virtue is not square I am *saying* anything different about virtue from what I am saying about my left eye when I say that my left eye is not square. In neither case am I *saying* anything whatever about what the object *is*, and in neither case am I saying *all* that it is not. In saying that my left eye is not square, I am not saying that it *is* of some other shape, and in saying that virtue is not square I am not saying that it is not of any other shape either; in both cases I am saying that the thing is not square, and that is *all* that I am saying.[2]

This view, that the negations of type crossings are true (and hence meaningful), has not gone completely unopposed in the literature. Arthur Pap has the following to say:

In ordinary parlance, a rejection of a statement of the form "x is blue" as false is equivalent to the assertion that x has some colour other than blue; similarly, were one to reject "x weighs more than y" as false, one would implicitly assert that either x and y have the same weight or y weighs more than x; and so on.[3]

I gather from this that Pap would take the sentence "the theory of relativity is not blue" to be equivalent, in ordinary language, to the meaningless sentence "the theory of relativity has some colour other than blue". Similarly, "the number 5 does not weigh more than the number 6" would be equivalent to the meaningless sentence "the number 5 weighs less than, or the same as, the number 6". So, in general, according to Pap, the negations of type crossings are meaningless rather than true, provided that their predicates are taken in the way they would

[2] A. N. Prior, "Entities", *The Australasian Journal of Philosophy*, XXXII (1954), pp. 159-160.
[3] Arthur Pap, "Types and Meaninglessness", *Mind*, LXIX (1960), p. 41.

normally be understood in ordinary language.[4] I think Pap is wrong on this point, and I shall try to explain why.

If an ordinary person were to be confronted by a sentence such as "the theory of relativity is not blue", it is not clear how he would react. Perhaps he would ask, as Pap suggests, "So what color is it, then?", and this might indicate that he takes the sentence to be meaningless. On the other hand, I could also see him as regarding the sentence to be true. Whatever answer the layman gives to the question whether the sentence is true or meaningless, very little would be shown about ordinary language, for the question is a philosophical question. The layman cannot be expected to reflect ordinary language, as opposed to philosophical language, if he is asked a philosophical question. All that would be shown by his answer is his particular way of thinking. For example, if he were to say of the sentence "the theory of relativity is not blue" that it is *true*, all this would show is that he has a certain uninhibited way of thinking: he does not read anything into statements, but takes them at face value, trying not to make unwarranted assumptions. On the other hand, if he says that the sentence is *meaningless*, all this shows is that he tends to think in terms of realms of discourse. He is making the unwarranted assumption that the sentence in question is within the realm of "physical object discourse" in which everything has some color or other. This shows that he has a somewhat inhibited way of thinking, tending to jump to unwarranted conclusions. (It was specifically against such a way of thinking that Prior directed his passage.) But nothing is shown here about ordinary language or ordinary usage. It may very well be a fact that in ordinary *life* no one who is speaking truthfully ever says of anything that it is not blue unless he believes it to have some color other than blue.

---

[4] In the same article (pp. 53-54), Pap allowed that the terms 'true', 'false', and 'meaningless' might be taken in a different way from ordinary language, so that the negations of type crossings might, in this new usage, be called "true" rather than "meaningless". But this is not relevant to the issue, for when Ewing and Prior apply truth to the negations of type crossings, it is clear that they intend to do so in accordance with ordinary language.

But it in no way follows from this that in ordinary *usage* 'x is not blue' entails 'x has some color other than blue'. Anyone who draws such an inference does so, not by virtue of any rules of ordinary language, but by virtue of his tendency to jump to unwarranted conclusions. Hence, no appeal to the reactions of ordinary people to the negations of type crossings could prove that such sentences are meaningless rather than true. In thinking that this could be proved, Pap was definitely mistaken.

Another objection to the Ewing-Prior position might be based on the principle (maintained by many philosophers, including Pap) that if a sentence is meaningless, then its negation must also be meaningless. On the basis of this principle, one might argue that the negations of type crossings must be meaningless, since type crossings themselves are. Pap did not explicitly state this argument in order to establish his point, but it seems to have strongly influenced his position on the matter.

Pap gave what he believed to be a satisfactory proof of the principle that if a sentence is meaningless, then its negation is meaningless. He says:

> ... the negation of a meaningless sentence is surely itself meaningless: the relevant sense of "meaningless" here is "neither true nor false", and by the principles of excluded middle and non-contradiction, if p is either true or false, then not-p is true or false; by contraposition, if not-p is neither true nor false, then p is neither true nor false.[5]

This proof contains several minor flaws[6] on which we need not

---

[5] *Ibid.,* p. 43.

[6] One flaw is that the terms 'meaningful' and 'meaningless' are applied to propositions, represented by the symbols 'p' and 'not-p'. But propositions are not linguistic entities, and therefore cannot be said to *have* meanings. On the contrary, they are usually said to *be* the meanings of (declarative) sentences. Another flaw in the argument is that it is not clear how the principles of excluded middle and non-contradiction, to which the proof appeals, are to be expressed. They cannot be expressed in the usual way, that is: "every sentence is either true or false" and "no sentence is both true and false", for, by the definition of 'meaningless' given in the

dwell. The real basis of the proof is the definition of 'meaning-less' as 'neither true nor false'. Given such a definition, it would follow, not only that the negation of a meaningless sentence is itself meaningless, but also that if type crossings are meaningless, then they are not false. However, I do not accept Pap's defini-tion, and when I said of type crossings that they are meaningless, I did not intend to say that they are neither true nor false. Pap's definition is a poor one, because when philosophers assert that false sentences are not meaningless, they invariably have in mind *empirically* false sentences. Therefore, a better definition of 'meaningless' would be 'neither true nor empirically false'. By this definition, a sentence could be meaningless even though its negation is not meaningless. And type crossings would be mea-ingless, since they are neither true nor empirically false.

There is no reason to accept Pap's definition of 'meaningless', nor is there any reason to accept the principle that if a sentence is meaningless, then its negation must be meaningless. We can perfectly well understand what a person is saying when he utters the negation of a certain sentence without having to understand what he or someone else might be trying to say by uttering the sentence itself. Nowhere is this more evident than in the area of type crossings. To say, "Socrates is a color" makes no sense at all; to say, "Socrates is not a color (but a person)" makes per-fectly good sense. There could be point in saying something without there having to be point in denying it as well. Thus, a sentence could be meaningless even though its negation is not meaningless.

It seems, then, that neither of the two objections to the Ewing-Prior position, which are considered above, will stand up. Hence, there does not seem to be any good reason to suppose that the negations of type crossings are meaningless. On the other hand, there are positive reasons for saying that such sentences are

---

argument, these principles would be equivalent to: "every sentence is meaningful" and "no sentence is meaningless", both of which are obvi-ously false. Therefore, it is not clear how the principles in question are to be expressed or what they could be.

meaningful. First of all, they can be given a use in the teaching of language. For example, a philosopher's child might say, "I want to color that picture Socrates", and the child's mother might correct it by saying, "Socrates is not a color; Socrates is a person." This is good evidence that the sentence "Socrates is not a color" is meaningful. And the same sort of case might be developed for the negation of any type crossing.

Furthermore, the negations of type crossings must be meaningful because they can be *proved true*, à la Prior, by appeal to premises whose truth is itself beyond question. In addition to the proof which Prior gives, I can cite, as examples of such proofs, the following:

Proof A
(1) The theory of relativity is a theory.
(2) Theories are abstract entities.
(3) No abstract entities are concrete entities.[7]
(4) Only concrete entities are colored.
(5) Only colored entities are blue.
(6) Therefore, the theory of relativity is not blue.

Proof B
(1) Smells pertain to the olfactory sense.
(2) What pertains to the olfactory sense cannot have an auditory property.
(3) Being loud is an auditory property.
(4) Therefore, smells are not loud.

Proof C
(1) Moral perfection is a state of being.
(2) No number is a state of being.
(3) All prime numbers are numbers.
(4) Therefore, moral perfection is not a prime number.

---

[7] The term 'concrete' is here taken in the very broadest possible sense. I want to include as concrete entities, not only material objects, but also all forms of energy (lights, sounds, electrical impulses, etc.) and sensations (pains, after-images, etc.). It is intended that the class of concrete entities and the class of abstract entities exhaust the class of entities (or things which sentences might possibly be about).

In each proof the bottom line follows logically from the preceding lines, each of which is a true statement. Therefore, each proof is *sound* and thus establishes the truth of its conclusion. Considering the strength of these proofs, it seems undeniable that the negations of type crossings are true statements and, therefore, type crossings themselves may be legitimately characterized as false statements. Each proof may be regarded as establishing the falsity of a given type crossing.

What kind of false statements are type crossings? They are not empirical falsehoods, for no empirical evidence could ever disconfirm them or be relevant to their falsity. None of the premises used in Proofs A–C are empirical premises. Rather, they are a priori premises, known to be true independently of experience. So, since the falsity of type crossings can be established by appeal to a priori premises alone, it follows that type crossings must be a priori falsehoods.

It is now possible to see one important difference between type crossings and ordinary falsehoods: whereas type crossings are a priori, ordinary falsehoods are empirical. And this is indeed a difference in kind. Type crossings can be known to be false without having to appeal to any experience, apart from the experience required in understanding the form of the sentence and the individual words in it. But this is not so in the case of ordinary false sentences. For example, to know that the sentence "the blood of a squirrel is blue" is false, one must have certain experiences apart from the experiences required in the understanding of the sentence, such as seeing the blood of a squirrel (or hearing or reading about it). This is not so in the case of a type crossing, as for example, "the theory of relativity is blue". One can understand what the blood of a squirrel is without knowing whether or not it is blue; but anyone who understands what the theory of relativity is knows with certainty that it has no color at all, and is therefore not blue. Thus, experience is needed in the case of an ordinary false sentence, but not in the case of a type crossing.

Nevertheless, to say that type crossings are a priori falsehoods is to say only that they can be known to be false independently of empirical evidence. So the basis of their falsity does not lie in experience. But the big question still remains, then: what *is* the basis of their falsity if not experience? Or, alternatively, what is the basis of their meaninglessness? This will be the main problem of the book.

2.2. DEFINITIONAL FALSEHOOD

One possible answer to the problem is to say that type crossings are self-contradictory. This position has been held by two philosophers: A. C. Ewing and A. J. Baker.

Ewing says the following:

... the statement –quadratic equations attend race-meetings– is self-contradictory.
... even self-contradictory sentences are not meaningless. I think that –quadratic equations attend race-meetings– is a statement which we understand perfectly well and it is only because we understand it so well that we see it to be so obviously false.[8]

Baker says the following:

Statements like "Equality is easily annoyed", "Greenness is hexagonal" do involve category mistakes, but this is because they can be shown to lead to contradictions rather than because they can be read off at once as absurd.[9]

It is interesting to note that although Ewing and Baker apparently agree that type crossings are self-contradictory, they disagree on the question whether type crossings are meaningful. Ewing holds that they are meaningful; Baker holds that they are not. In this section, however, I shall take up only the question of whether or not type crossings are self-contradictory.

One philosopher who denies that type crossings are self-contradictory is P. F. Strawson. He says the following:

---

[8] A. C. Ewing, *op. cit.*, pp. 362-364. See also: Morris Lazerowitz, *The Structure of Metaphysics* (London, Routledge & Kegan Paul, 1955), pp. 248-249.
[9] A. J. Baker, "Category Mistakes", *Australasian Journal of Philosophy*, XXXIV (1956), p. 20.

Some have been tempted to assimilate violations of type-restrictions to self-contradictions. But this seems a mistake. The reason why 'loud smell' makes no sense is not that smells, like murmurs, are necessarily soft. Referring to something as a smell proscribes as senseless the question whether it is loud or not loud: it does not commit the speaker to one of two incompatible answers to the question.[10]

As an argument for the conclusion that "smells are loud" is not self-contradictory, this passage is certainly muddled and weak. Strawson's reason for believing that 'loud smell' is not self-contradictory, namely, that referring to something as a smell proscribes as senseless the question whether it is loud or not loud, seems not to constitute any reason at all. Consider this analogy: a "Wittgensteinian" might say that referring to someone as a bachelor proscribes as senseless the question whether he is married or not married. But this certainly would not commit him to the view that 'married bachelor' is not self-contradictory.

It might be possible to try to reconstruct Strawson's argument in either of the following two ways:

A: If a sentence is not senseless, then its denial is not senseless.
B: The sentence "smells are loud" is senseless.
C: Logically necessary sentences are not senseless.
D: Self-contradictory sentences are the denials of logically necessary sentences.
E: Therefore, the sentence "smells are loud" is not self-contradictory.

A: The sentence "smells are not loud" is senseless.
B: Logically necessary sentences are not senseless.
C: Self-contradictory sentences are the denials of logically necessary sentences.
D: Therefore, the sentence "smells are loud" is not self-contradictory.

In each case, however, although the conclusion does follow logically from the premises, the first premise (i.e., premise A) is

---

[10] P. F. Strawson, *Introduction to Logical Theory* (London, Methuen & Co., 1952), p. 227.

false. This point (that both first premises are false) was defended in Section 2.1, above. I can only conclude, then, that Strawson's attempt to show that type crossings are not self-contradictory is unsuccessful.

Nevertheless, it will be my contention that type crossings are not self-contradictory. To make the discussion more precise, however, I shall introduce the expression 'definitional falsehood' in place of the expression 'self-contradictory sentence'. Consider, then, the following definitions:

(1) 'Logical truth' = 'a sentence whose truth can be proved by appeal to the rules of logic alone'.
(2) 'Simple definitional truth' = 'a sentence which can be converted into a logical truth by substituting for (one or more) terms in the sentence the conventional definitions of those terms'.
(3) 'Definitional truth' = 'a sentence which is either a simple definitional truth or else one which follows logically from some set of simple definitional truths'.

Examples to illustrate these concepts are the following:

(a) Logical truth: "all male parents are parents".
(b) Simple definitional truth: "all fathers are parents".
(c) Non-simple definitional truth: "all fathers have children" (which follows logically from the simple definitional truths "all fathers are parents" and "all parents have children").

The expression 'definitional falsehood' may now be defined as 'the negation of a definitional truth'.

When I say that type crossings are not self-contradictory, what I mean is that they are not definitional falsehoods, as defined above.[11] There is a certain problem in defending this view in that no one has put forward any arguments to attack it. Those who

---

[11] I feel that my usage here is fairly standard. On the other hand, it may be that some philosophers, including Ewing and Baker, take the term 'self-contradictory' in a broader sense, so that 'x is self-contradictory' means something like 'x violates conventions of ordinary language'. The question of whether or not type crossings are self-contradictory in this broader sense will be taken up in Chapter 4.

claim that type crossings are self-contradictory, such as Ewing and Baker, have not, to my knowledge, attempted to support their claim by deriving any contradictions from type crossings. However, it is easy to see what sort of argument might be put forward. It might be argued, for example, that the premises of Proofs A–C (above) are all definitional truths. It would then follow that the type crossings which are the negations of their conclusions are definitional falsehoods. And furthermore, any type crossing at all could be shown to be a definitional falsehood by constructing a suitable set of premises in an analogous way.

To defend my view against this hypothetical attack, I shall argue, first of all, that in each of the Proofs A–C there is at least one premise which is not a definitional truth, and second, that, in general, the negations of type crossings cannot be proved by appeal to definitional truths alone. My conclusion will be that type crossings are not definitional falsehoods and that their falsity must therefore be based on something other than the way the terms in them are conventionally defined.

A certain requirement is placed on the definition of a term in order for it to be usable in a proof that a given sentence containing the term is a definitional truth. The requirement is that the definition state the *conventional* connotation of the term being defined. In other words, it must indicate those properties the possession or lack of which constitutes the conventional criterion by which we decide whether an object is or is not denoted by the term. For example, a definition of 'triangle' as 'a plane figure the sum of whose interior angles equals 180 degrees' would not meet the requirement, whereas the definition 'a plane figure enclosed by exactly three straight lines' would meet the requirement, for only the latter property constitutes the conventional connotation of the term 'triangle'. There may be people who know what triangles are but who do not know that they have the former property; but this could not be true of the latter property because it is that which we use to decide of a given figure whether or not it is a triangle.

On the basis of this restriction, it can be quite plausibly argued that in each of the Proofs A–C there is at least one premise which is not a definitional truth. Proof A has two premises which I should want to deny are definitional truths. These are premises (2) and (4). In premise (2), theories are classified as being abstract entities, and in premise (4), colored entities are classified as being concrete entities. Now, the definitions of the terms 'theory' and 'colored' are admittedly a matter of debate. However, surely no one ever has or ever will define them in such a way that premises (2) and (4) are definitional truths. It is true that people who understand the terms involved would agree that theories are necessarily abstract entities and that colored things are necessarily concrete entities. But this is not to say that people *conventionally define* 'theory' and 'colored' in terms of those classes. The term 'theory' might be defined as 'a coherent group of general propositions used as principles of explanation for a class of phenomena', but not as 'such-and-such a type of abstract entity'; similarly, the term 'colored' might be defined as 'having that quality of a visual sensation distinct from form', but not as 'being such-and-such a type of concrete entity'. It seems, then, that premises (2) and (4) could never be shown to be true by appeal to conventional definitions alone. It follows that they are not definitional truths.

In Proof B, the premise which I want to deny is a definitional truth is premise (2). It reads: "What pertains to the olfactory sense cannot have an auditory property". This sentence is of such a structure that it is not clear how anyone could even attempt to transform it into a logical truth through the use of conventional definitions. The words 'olfactory' and 'auditory' are not defined negatively in terms of one another. 'Olfactory' is conventionally defined as 'pertaining to the sense of smell', 'auditory', as 'pertaining to the sense of hearing'. And the terms 'smell' and 'hearing' are again conventionally defined in a positive way, not in a negative way. I think it is clear from this that premise (2) is not a definitional truth.

In Proof C, it is again premise (2) which is not a definitional truth. Premise (2) reads: "No number is a state of being". Here again, it seems that in order for the sentence to be capable of being transformed into a logical truth through the use of conventional definitions, those definitions would have to be negative in character. But the words 'number', 'state', and 'being' are positive rather than negative. 'Number', for example, might be defined as a certain type of class, but not as something which (among other things) is not a state of being. It seems, then, that premise (2) cannot be proved by appeal to conventional definitions alone. It is therefore something other than a definitional truth.

Now, from the fact that Proofs A–C each contain at least one premise which is not a definitional truth, it does not follow that their conclusions are not definitional truths. However, this would follow if it could be shown that those premises which are not definitional truths are essential to any proofs for the conclusions of Proofs A–C. To establish this point, I shall first separate type crossings into three different groups.

First of all, some type crossings predicate of concrete entities properties which apply only to abstract entities; and some type crossings predicate of abstract entities properties which apply only to concrete entities. Let us call all such type crossings as these "concrete-abstract type crossings". Of our original eight type crossings, the first four are of this sort. For example, sentence (4) ("quadruplicity drinks procrastination") predicates of the abstract entities, quadruplicity and procrastination, the relation (or "two-place property") of drinking, which applies only to concrete entities.

There are also type crossings which predicate of one type of concrete entity a property which applies only to another type of concrete entity. Type crossings (5) and (6) ("smells are loud" and "I have eaten a loud clap") are both of this sort. Sentence (6), for example, predicates of the pair of concrete entities, I and a loud clap, the relation of eating, which applies only to another type of (pair of) concrete entities. Let us call such sentences "intra-concrete type crossings".

Finally, there are type crossings which predicate of one type of abstract entity a property which applies only to another type of abstract entity. Let us call these "intra-abstract type crossings". Examples would be type crossings (7) and (8) ("moral perfection is a prime number" and "chemistry is a greater ordinal than the concept of truth").

Of course, these distinctions are not at all clear-cut, for the concepts on which they are based, abstract entity and concrete entity, are quite imprecise. But they are useful distinctions, nevertheless.

Now we can raise the question: how can the negation of a concrete-abstract type crossing be proved? The answer seems clear: by showing that the subject designates an abstract entity, whereas the positive predicate [12] is applicable only to concrete entities (or vice versa). That is, in order for the premises of the proof to be explicit, some appeal must be made to classification in terms of the concepts of an abstract entity and a concrete entity. But then we can see that, in Proof A, premises (2) and (4) are quite essential. The conclusion could not have been established without them, that is, without either appealing to them explicitly or else presupposing them. And since those premises are not definitional truths, it follows that the conclusion of Proof A is not a definitional truth. Furthermore, since any proof for the negation of a concrete-abstract type crossing must rely on classifications in terms of the concepts of an abstract entity and a concrete entity, and since such classifications are never part of (nor follow from) conventional definitions, it follows that the negations of concrete-abstract type crossings can never be proved by appeal to conventional definitions alone. They are therefore not definitional truths. Hence, concrete-abstract type crossings are not definitional falsehoods.

However, there seems to be an exception to this generalization in the following sentence:

[12] All negations of type crossings have a negative term in them. By 'positive predicate' I mean the predicate without that negative term. Thus, the positive predicate in "the theory is not blue" is 'is blue'; the positive predicate in "quadruplicity does not drink procrastination" is 'drinks' or 'does drink' (a "two-place predicate").

(11) An abstract entity is a concrete entity.

It might plausibly be argued that 'abstract' is conventionally defined in a negative way, as 'conceived apart from matter and from special cases', and that 'concrete' could be taken to mean 'conceived in terms of matter or special cases'. On the basis of such definitions, (11) could be proved to be a definitional falsehood. That it is a definitional falsehood I shall not deny. After all, even if the suggested definitions can be criticized, it still must be acknowledged that 'abstract' and 'concrete' are conventionally defined in opposition to each other. Sentence (11), then, together with any sentence based on the same idea (such as "some abstract entities are concrete entities", "all concrete entities are abstract entities", etc.), must be a definitional falsehood.

However, that (11) should be called a "concrete-abstract type crossing" is not quite so clear. Are we to say that the expressions 'abstract entity' and 'concrete entity' designate types of thing? We could say that they do only if we keep in mind that they are the very broadest possible classes that could constitute types of thing. Nevertheless, apart from the extreme generality of the categories involved, (11) seems to be like sentences (1)–(8). Although it is by no means a clear case, it might conceivably be called a concrete-abstract type crossing. Therefore, I shall admit that there is *one* type crossing that is a definitional falsehood. But it is the only one. Sentence (11) is a special isolated case in that 'abstract entity' is probably the only expression in the English language which is conventionally defined in a negative way and which also designates what may properly be called a "type of thing".[13]

Let us now turn from concrete-abstract type crossings to intra-concrete type crossings. The only way for the negation of an intra-concrete type crossing to be proved is by showing that the

[13] Having mentioned this one exception, I shall proceed to disregard it, so as not to burden the discussion which follows. I do not regard the exception as very important, because it is far from being a clear case of a type crossing. Furthermore, see p. 110 below.

positive predicate is not applicable to the type of concrete entity represented by the subject. It seems, then, that in every proof for the negation of an intra-concrete type crossing there must be (either presupposed or explicitly stated) a premise to the effect that the type of thing represented by the subject does *not* have a certain property or is *not* included in a certain class of things. But then we can see that, in Proof B, premise (2) is quite essential. The conclusion could not have been obtained without an appeal to such a premise. But such premises are never definitional truths, for expressions which designate *concrete* types of thing are always conventionally defined in a positive way rather than in a negative way (i.e. by stating what the thing *is* rather than what it is not). It follows from this, not only that the conclusion of Proof B is not a definitional truth, but that the negations of intra-concrete type crossings are never definitional truths. Hence, intra-concrete type crossings are never definitional falsehoods.

These same considerations apply to Proof C and to intra-abstract type crossings, for, by the same reasoning, it could be shown that every proof for the negation of an intra-abstract type crossing must rely upon a premise which states that the type of thing represented by the subject does *not* have a certain property or is *not* included in a certain class of things. And since such premises are never definitional truths, it follows, not only that the conclusion of Proof C is not a definitional truth, but that the negations of intra-abstract type crossings are never definitional truths. Hence, intra-abstract type crossings are never definitional falsehoods.

By showing that no concrete-abstract, intra-concrete, or intra-abstract type crossings are definitional falsehoods, I hope to have shown that no type crossings at all are definitional falsehoods, for every type crossing must be of one of those three groups.

However, it might be objected that the following sentences constitute counter-examples:

(12) Prime numbers are not numbers.

(13) An entity which is not a number is a number.

It is true that both of these sentences are definitional falsehoods.[14] But I should certainly want to deny that they are type crossings. Originally, we defined type crossings to be sentences which are like sentences (1)–(8) in that they say of one type of thing something that has application only to another type of thing. But (12) and (13) are not of this sort at all. Sentence (12) asserts of one type of thing that it is *not* that type of thing. But to assert this is not to assert anything that has application to any particular type of thing, whereas sentences (1)–(8) do each assert something that has application to a particular type of thing. On these grounds, (12) can be said to be sufficiently unlike (1)–(8) to be denied classification as a type crossing. Sentence (13), on the other hand, asserts of things which are not of a given type that they are of that type. But there is nothing about the class of things which are not of a given type that warrants saying that it is itself a type of thing. Therefore, sentence (13) says nothing about a type of thing, and so, is clearly unlike (1)–(8). It follows that neither (12) nor (13) should be called a "type crossing" at all.

My conclusion to this section, then, is that although type crossings are a priori falsehoods, the basis of their a priori falsity does not lie in conventional definitions. They are not self-contradictory in the sense of being definitional falsehoods. So we are still left with the problem of explaining just what the basis of their a priori falsity really is.

It must be pointed out here that there are sentences other than type crossings which are likewise false a priori, but not definitional falsehoods. The following may be cited as examples:

(14) Some red things are all green.

(15) Temporal precedence is a symmetrical relation.

---

[14] Actually, they are logical falsehoods (the negations of logical truths) and are therefore definitional falsehoods in a trivial way. That is, they are definitional falsehoods because the fact that their negations follow logically from *any* set of premises entails that their negations follow logically from some set of simple definitional truths.

(16) There exist in the universe an object and a cube such that the object is moving in a direction perpendicular to each of three adjacent edges of the cube at the same time.

These sentences are not definitional falsehoods because there is no way in which their negations could be derived from simple definitional truths alone. They are a priori falsehoods because their negations can be known to be true independently of experience. But they are not type crossings, for they do not say of one type of thing something that has application only to another *type* of thing. Thus, the question arises as to what, precisely, is the difference between type crossings and these other sentences. This is indeed a knotty problem, and one which, to my knowledge, has hitherto gone unnoticed in the literature of philosophy and linguistics.

In the process of solving this knotty problem, we will need to solve one of our other major problems, namely, "what exactly is a type crossing?"

GRAMMAR

3.1. TYPE CROSSINGS RESTRICTED

Before proceeding further in our investigations, it will be necessary for us to make the concept of a type crossing more precise by placing two restrictions on it. The first restriction is that type crossings be composed solely of English words.[1] This I shall refer to as "the vocabulary requirement". The second restriction is a bit more complicated and will take more space to develop. I shall lead up to it by means of the following discussion.

Most English sentences which are uttered in everyday life and which are heard on the radio or read in magazines, etc. are clearly meaningful sentences in the sense that almost all native speakers of English would understand them, even if they were to occur in isolation (as, say, in the case where they are written on scraps of paper). I shall refer to such sentences as "clearly meaningful sentences". An example of one would be the following:

(17) The sky is blue.

---

[1] The present book is completely relativized to combinations of English words. Thus, a more precise title for it would be "English Type Crossings", rather than just "Type Crossings". Although type crossings can be formulated in most other languages, I am not at all sure that the results which I shall obtain with respect to English type crossings would also apply to them. Therefore, it must be understood that the statements I make about what I call "type crossings" are meant to apply only to English type crossings. And the same applies to my use of the terms 'sentence' and 'sequence'.

The formulation of a general theory of type crossings – applicable to all languages – would be of considerable interest and significance. For example, it would be of great interest to learn whether there are natural languages in which type crossings cannot be formulated at all. Needless to say, such an endeavor is beyond the scope of the present book.

On the other hand, the following two sequences of words are something other than clearly meaningful sentences:

(18) The theory is blue.

(19) The theory is but.[2]

Sequence (18) is a type crossing. But what about (19)? The inclination is to say that (19) is not a type crossing, for it is not even a sentence, but a series of words arranged in an ungrammatical way. Type crossings are supposed to say of one type of thing something that has application only to another type of thing. But (19) does not do this, for the expression 'is but' has no application to anything.

In language, things are designated by noun morphemes. One may infer, then, that if a sentence says of one type of thing something that has application only to another type of thing, then it must be possible to transform the sentence into a clearly meaningful sentence by substituting for at least one of the noun morphemes in it a different noun morpheme. This point is illustrated by sentences (17) and (18). Sentence (18), which is a type crossing, can be transformed into the clearly meaningful sentence (17) by replacing the noun morpheme 'theory' by the noun morpheme 'sky'. However, sequence (19) cannot be transformed in this way because there is no noun morpheme at all to which the expression 'is but' can be significantly joined.

This, then, is the second restriction to be placed upon type crossings. It may be stated as a necessary condition: in order for a sequence to be a type crossing it is necessary that it be capable of being transformed into a clearly meaningful sentence by substituting for at least one of the noun morphemes in it a different noun morpheme. Since (19) does not meet this requirement, (19) is not a type crossing.

It should be mentioned that the substitution here referred to may be a plural substitution (i.e. a group of noun morphemes for another group). Consider, for example, the sentence "quadruplicity drinks procrastination". By substituting for the noun mor-

---

[2] Here, it is to be understood that the word 'but' is indeed the English conjunction 'but'.

phemes 'quadruplicity' and 'procrastination' the noun morphemes 'Jones' and 'beer', we arrive at the clearly meaningful sentence "Jones drinks beer". This is to be taken as a case of conformity with the criterion. Hence, "quadruplicity drinks procrastination" meets the given requirement for being a type crossing.

Having introduced the requirement, it will now be necessary to revise it. What must be done is to take account of noun phrases, such as, for example, 'the theory of relativity'. As the requirement now stands, it may very well be that our prime example of a type crossing, "the theory of relativity is blue", will turn out to be not a type crossing, since there may not be any clearly meaningful sentence having the form "the —— of —— is blue". Certainly we should not have to search for a meaningful sentence of *that* form in order to show that "the theory of relativity is blue" is a type crossing. All we should have to search for is a meaningful sentence of the form "—— is blue", where we may put into the blank, not only a noun morpheme, but also what I shall call a "regular noun phrase".

I propose to use the term 'noun phrase' to mean 'a noun morpheme together with its modifiers'. Thus, 'the theory of relativity' is a noun phrase because it consists of a noun morpheme, 'theory', together with two modifiers, 'the' and the prepositional phrase 'of relativity'. I shall also intend the same remarks which I made about clearly meaningful sentences to be applied to noun phrases, so that noun phrases, too, can be "clearly meaningful".

Now, by a "regular noun phrase" I shall mean a noun phrase which is either clearly meaningful or which can be converted into a clearly meaningful noun phrase by substituting for at least one of the noun morphemes in it a different noun morpheme. Examples of noun phrases which are regular in this sense are the following:

the theory of relativity
a green number
a brightly wrapped number.

Examples of noun phrases which are not regular are the following:

a brightly number
a brightly large number.

We may now revise our restriction on type crossings to read as follows:

In order for a sequence to be a type crossing it is necessary that it be capable of being transformed into a clearly meaningful sentence by substituting for at least one of the noun morphemes or regular noun phrases in it a different noun morpheme or regular noun phrase.

I shall want to claim that all sentences which we are inclined to say involve a crossing of types of *things* meet this requirement, including sentences such as:

The theory of relativity is blue.
A green number is valid.
A brightly wrapped number is valid.

The requirement is therefore adequate as a necessary condition for type crossings.

Two sequences which are eliminated from the class of type crossings by the requirement in question are the following:

(20) Jones saw the book carefully.
(21) The package is brightly large.

Neither of these sequences can be transformed into a clearly meaningful sentence by substitution of one noun morpheme or regular noun phrase for another. Instead of crossing types of *things,* they seem to involve a crossing of some other kinds of types. But, until we get to Chapter 8, I shall restrict the term 'type crossing' to crossings of types of things. Hence, even though (20) and (21) each involve a crossing of some kind of types, they are not to be called "type crossings" in the sense in which I shall use that term through Chapter 7.

One of my reasons for restricting the scope of Chapters 1–7 in this way is that the vast majority of philosophers who have

written about type crossings (or used them as examples) have
done so with respect to type crossings in the restricted sense, as
defined above.[3] They seem to have had in common the notion of a
type crossing as a sentence which says of one type of *thing* something that has application only to another type of *thing*. It is that
notion, and the views which have been held about it, which I
want to examine first. In Chapter 8, a broader notion of type
crossing will be introduced, one in which sequences (20) and
(21) *would* count as type crossings.

Consider, now, the following two sequences:

(22) There are three golds in the yard.

(23) There are three gold in the yard.

A discussion of these two sequences will provide further elucida-
tion of the requirements set on type crossings above, for I shall
maintain that neither of them is a type crossing. Sequence (22)
is not a type crossing because the symbol 'golds' is not a word of
English, hence, (22) violates the vocabulary requirement. On

---

[3]   To illustrate this point, here is a list of several philosophers, in addition to those mentioned elsewhere in the book, who have made reference
to type crossings. I have also indicated the examples they have used:

(1) Rudolph Carnap, "Testability and Meaning",   "This stone is now think-
Philosophy of Science, IV (1937), p. 5.   ing about Vienna"

(2) Victor Kraft, *The Vienna Circle* (New York,   "Caesar is a prime num-
Philosophical Library, 1953), p. 34.   ber"

(3) John Passmore, *Philosophical Reasoning*   "My kangaroo is the fifth
(New York, Charles Scribner's Sons, 1961),   day of the week"
p. 141.

(4) Hans Reichenbach, *Elements of Symbolic*   "Caesar is a prime num-
Logic (New York, Macmillan Co., 1947), p. 7.   ber"

(5) Bertrand Russell, *An Inquiry into Meaning*   "Quadruplicity drinks
and Truth (London, Allen and Unwin, Ltd.,   procrastination"
1940), p. 166.

(6) Michael Shorter, "Meaning and Grammar",   "Virtue is blue"
Australasian Journal of Philosophy, XXXIV
(1956), p. 73.

(7) Wilbur M. Urban, *Language and Reality*   "Caesar is a prime num-
(London, Allen and Unwin, Ltd., 1939), p. 198.   ber"

In addition to being an illustration, this list should provide some useful
references on type crossings in the philosophical literature.

the other hand, the reason (23) is not a type crossing is that it cannot be transformed into a clearly meaningful sentence by substitution of one noun morpheme or regular noun phrase for another. The reason behind this is that the substitution of a plural noun or noun phrase for a singular noun or noun phrase involves the addition of the plurality morpheme, which is neither a noun morpheme nor a noun phrase nor part of such. For example, the substitution of 'boys' for 'gold' would not be just substitution of noun morpheme for noun morpheme (as would be the substitution of 'boy' for 'gold'); it would be the substitution of two morphemes, 'boy' and the plurality morpheme, for one morpheme. This, then, would not satisfy the criterion which was stated previously. And the same applies to the substitution of, say, 'pieces of gold' for 'gold'; this would involve the substitution of a noun phrase, 'piece of gold', plus the plurality morpheme for a noun morpheme, which, again, would not satisfy the criterion. But, now, suppose we were to substitute the word 'deer' for 'gold', getting the sentence "there are three deer in the yard". Has a plurality morpheme been added here? It might be argued that the resulting sentence is clearly meaningful only if the word 'deer' is understood as plural; if 'deer' is understood as singular, then the sentence is not clearly meaningful. In light of these considerations, I shall maintain that when we substitute 'deer' for 'gold' and get a clearly meaningful sentence, the substitution still does not satisfy our criterion, for a plurality morpheme has been introduced in addition to the noun morpheme. It may be a plurality morpheme that is only tacit or understood,[4] but it must

---

[4] It may be that this talk about "tacit morphemes" constitutes too great a departure from the standard use of the word 'morpheme' among linguists. In this case, I would have to go back and revise our restriction to read as follows:

In order for a sequence to be a type crossing it is necessary that it be capable of being transformed into a clearly meaningful sentence by substituting for at least one of the noun morphemes or regular noun phrases in it a different noun morpheme or regular noun phrase of the same number (i.e., singular or plural) as the original.

When it is stated in this way, it is quite clear that sequence (23) does *not* meet the restriction.

have been added in order for the resulting sentence to be clearly meaningful. It seems, then, that since there is no way to transform (23) into a clearly meaningful sentence by substitution of one noun morpheme or regular noun phrase for another, it cannot qualify as a type crossing. Instead of saying of one type of thing something that has application only to another type of thing, (23) says of one thing (viz., the substance gold) something that has application only to a *set of things*.

It is important to understand that the criterion introduced above is only a necessary condition for being a type crossing, not a sufficient condition. There are many sentences which satisfy it, but which are not type crossings. In fact, every meaningful sentence of English satisfies it. The purpose of the criterion is not to distinguish type crossings from meaningful sentences, but to distinguish them from sequences such as (19)–(23). Thus, inasmuch as the two requirements put forward in this section constitute only a necessary condition for being a type crossing, and not a sufficient condition, they are at best only *part* of a theory of type crossings. However, they do clarify the concept of a type crossing sufficiently for the purposes of the present chapter.

3.2. SENTENCE STRUCTURE

It is my purpose in this chapter to defend the view held by many philosophers[5] that type crossings are grammatical and therefore properly referred to as "sentences". But I propose to do this without having to formulate a definition of 'grammatical', which would be a difficult undertaking. The basis of my argument is the principle that, since all clearly meaningful sentences are grammatical, if a sequence can be transformed into a clearly meaningful sentence without at all changing its *structure*, then

---

[5] Victor Kraft, Hans Reichenbach, Bertrand Russell, Gilbert Ryle, P. F. Strawson, to name just a few. (For references on these, see note 3 in this chapter, and notes 1 and 7 in the next chapter.)

the sequence must be grammatical. For example, it can be plausibly claimed that sequence (14) ("some red things are all green") is a grammatical sequence, since it can be transformed into the clearly meaningful sentence "some round things are all green" and this sentence has exactly the same structure as the original sequence.[6] On the other hand, a sequence such as (19) ("the theory is but") has a structure so peculiar [7] that no sequence having the same structure could possibly be a meaningful sentence. Therefore (19) could not be proved to be grammatical on the basis of the principle in question.

In the previous section it was stipulated that all type crossings can be transformed into clearly meaningful sentences by substitution of at least one noun morpheme or regular noun phrase for another. But, according to our principle, anything that can be transformed into a clearly meaningful sentence without any change in structure must be grammatical. Therefore, it would be possible to prove that all type crossings are grammatical if it could be shown that the transformation of an English sequence into a clearly meaningful sentence by substitution of one noun morpheme or regular noun phrase for another never results in a change in structure.

I believe this last point can be plausibly defended. We can begin by noting that two kinds of expressions occur in English

[6] The structure could be represented in various ways. A grammarian might read off what he takes to be the grammatical classes of the individual words, possibly as follows: quantificational adjective, descriptive adjective, plural noun, copula, quantificational adverb, descriptive adjective. On the other hand, a logician might represent the structure as follows: $(E x)(Rx \ \& \ (y)(Pyx \supset Gy))$, where 'Pyx' represents 'y is a part of x', 'Gy' represents 'y is green', and 'Rx' represents either 'x is red' or 'x is round'. In any case, no matter how the structure is represented, both sentences will be taken to have the same structure.

[7] The grammatical classes read off as: definite article, noun, copula, conjunction. Anything ending in a conjunction is of course grammatically incomplete or ungrammatical. As far as the logical form goes, it is not clear how one might even attempt to symbolize it. The closest I can come, using 'a' to represent the theory referred to, would be the following: &a. Naturally, such a sequence would not be a well-formed formula of any symbolic system or language.

sequences: function expressions and content expressions. Function expressions are the grammatical forms which determine the
structure of a sentence. They, so to speak, provide the skeleton
of a sentence, whereas content expressions fill in the flesh. But
all noun morphemes and regular noun phrases of English are
content expressions; they are never function expressions. Therefore, they do not determine in any way the structure of a sequence. All of these points have been defended by modern logicians[8] and linguists.[9]

Since the structure of an English sequence is not determined by
the noun morphemes or regular noun phrases which it contains,
it follows that substitution of one noun morpheme or regular
noun phrase for another in an English sequence will not change
its structure. Therefore, the possibility of substituting one noun
morpheme or regular noun phrase for another in a given English
sequence and thereby producing a clearly meaningful sentence
is a sufficient condition for the grammaticality[10] of that sequence.

[8]   I have in mind such references as Rudolph Carnap, *The Logical Syntax
of Language* (New York, The Humanities Press, Inc., 1937) and W. V. O.
Quine, *Mathematical Logic* (Cambridge, Harvard University Press, 1955).
Logicians regularly replace nouns by arbitrary letters when they symbolize
sentences; but conjunctions, pronouns, the verb 'to be', and so on, cannot
be replaced in any arbitrary way. The reason for this, they would claim,
is that nouns are not part of the basic form of a sentence (the sentence
frame), but are what the form is filled with. And for the purposes of filling
the form, any distinctions among them are irrelevant.

[9]   C. F. Hockett, *A Course in Modern Linguistics* (New York, The
Macmillan Co., 1958), pp. 261-267. What I have said about the distinction
between function expressions and content expressions is an oversimplifi-
cation. In the pages cited, Hockett gives a much more precise and detailed
account of the distinction.

[10]   Noam Chomsky, in his book *Syntactic Structures* (volume 4 of the
Janua Linguarum series), formulates the noun as 'grammaticalness'. However, 'grammaticality' is closer to English usage. Note such words as
'practical' – 'practicality', 'spherical' – 'sphericality', etc.
   It is interesting to note a certain pattern in the literature with respect
to these words. All those who agree with Chomsky's views on type crossings formulate the noun as 'grammaticalness'. For example, see D. J. Hillman, "On Grammars and Category Mistakes", *Mind*, LXXII (1963), and
Paul Ziff, "About Ungrammaticalness', *Mind*, LXXIII (1964). On the
other hand, Chomsky's critics formulate the noun as 'grammaticality'. For

But it is also a necessary condition for that sequence to be a type crossing. It follows from this that if a sequence is a type crossing, it must be grammatical.

This result is quite in accord with the concept of grammaticality in ordinary language. I have questioned ordinary people on this point and they invariably said of type crossings that they *are* grammatical, whereas sequences such as (19) are ungrammatical. Of course, this sort of evidence is not conclusive because the concept of grammaticality is a semi-technical concept, and there is no good reason to believe that ordinary people have a mastery of its use. Paul Ziff puts it this way:

> Some seem to think that since they weren't taught at school not to say 'He had a green thought', there's nothing ungrammatical about the sentence. The sentence is grammatical according to the grammar they learned at school, so the sentence is grammatical.
>
> ... But is the grammar they learned at school a correct grammar of English? [11]

Ziff goes on to argue that the grammar learned at shool is not a correct grammar because it is too coarse. A finer concept is called-for. Certainly we can agree with Ziff that the so-called parts of speech are not sufficient as grammatical classes (or grammatical categories). Consider, for example, the following sequences:

(24) He is have were.
(25) Their think whose is whatever.
(26) Smith although Jones spoke until not Brown.

By substitution of verbs for verbs, (24) can be transformed into the meaningful sentence "he may have come". By substitution of pronouns for pronouns, (25) can be transformed into the meaningful sentence "I think that is him." And by substitution

---

example, see Archibald A. Hill, "Grammaticality", *Word,* XVII (1961), and Jerrold J. Katz, "Semi-sentences", printed in *The Structure of Language,* ed. Jerry A. Fodor & Jerrold J. Katz (Englewood Cliffs, Prentice-Hall, Inc., 1964).

[11]   Paul Ziff, *op. cit.,* pp. 204-205.

of conjunctions for conjunctions, (26) can be transformed into the meaningful sentence "Smith and Jones spoke but not Brown". Yet, (24)–(26) are admittedly ungrammatical. Even those with the most coarse notion of grammar would regard them as ungrammatical. It follows that the parts of speech, verb, pronoun, conjunction, etc., cannot be our only grammatical classes, for if they were, then (24)–(26) would have to be regarded as grammatical. It is clear that the parts of speech have to be divided into subclasses and these subclasses regarded as the true grammatical classes, and that this must be done in such a way that sequences such as (24)–(26) turn out to be ungrammatical.

However, Ziff wants to go further and divide the class of *nouns* into mutually exclusive subclasses in such a way that even type crossings (e.g., "he had a green thought") would turn out to be ungrammatical.[12] The question then arises as to whether such a division of nouns is purely arbitrary (or *ad hoc*) or whether there could be some basis for it. Certainly there is a difference in type between a thought and, say, a hat. But is this a difference in grammatical structure or a difference between two kinds of content words? Are the two sentences "he has a thought" and "he has a hat" different in their grammatical structure? It is very hard to say that they are. There seems to be no good reason at all to say that the difference is a grammatical one. Ziff says that the subclasses of nouns to which he appeals are of use in "a transformational analysis of English".[13] But, even if that is true, I fail to see the relevance of it. I see no reason why a correct grammar of English should have to rely on a transformational analysis.

Consider this sentence:

(27) A person's thoughts are in his brain.

Interpreted literally, (27) is a type crossing. But I cannot see how we could charge it with being ungrammatical, except in some purely metaphorical sense of 'grammaticality'. If an English

---

[12]   *Ibid.*, p. 214.
[13]   *Ibid.*, p. 214.

teacher were to warn his students that he would deduct 5 points from their papers for every lapse from correct grammar, it would be quite unfair of him to deduct the 5 points for sentence (27). This holds for most of the conceptual absurdities that one encounters in students' papers, such as "the truth of a moral judgement is emotive", " '2 plus 2 equals 4' is a valid argument", etc. (as well as type crossings of an even more subtle sort, such as "$\sqrt{3}$ is a prime number"). Type crossings of this sort, or any other sort, do involve conceptual absurdities, but not lapses from correct grammar. There is no reason to contradict our ordinary intuitions by saying that type crossings are ungrammatical. To do so, I suspect, involves passing from our ordinary notion of grammar to a kind of *metaphorical* notion, analogous to that suggested by Ludwig Wittgenstein in his remarks about the "logical grammar" of expressions.

The advocate of dividing nouns into grammatical subclasses may make one last stab with the important distinction between count nouns and mass nouns. Ziff says the following:

> The word 'chicken' in English falls under the category *Count Noun* and also under the category *Mass Noun*, and thus under the disjunctive category *Count/Mass Noun*, all of which are proper subcategories of the category *Noun*. The relevant difference between mass nouns and count nouns is that the former requires neither an article nor a plural affix. Thus the sentence 'It's nice to have chicken' and the sentences 'It's nice to have a chicken' and 'It's nice to have chickens' are all grammatical. But if 'tree' is simply a count noun and not a mass noun, and if these categories have a degree of utility equal to or greater than n, the sentence 'It's nice to have tree' is ungrammatical.[14]

Let us consider this latter sequence:

(28) It's nice to have tree.

I agree with Ziff that (28) is ungrammatical and that the class of nouns needs to be divided into the subclasses of count nouns and mass nouns in order to yield the true grammatical classes of English. But the question arises: is (28) a type crossing? It must

[14]   *Ibid.,* **pp.** 211-212.

be recalled that a type crossing is supposed to be a sentence that says of one type of thing something that has application only to another type of thing. Does (28) fit this description? It might be argued that trees are "count things" rather than "mass things" (where these expressions are defined along the lines suggested by Ziff). Thus, (28) says of a count thing something that has application only to a mass thing. And since count things and mass things are different types of thing, it follows that (28) is a type crossing.

I want to object to this argument on the grounds that (28) does *not* say anything of any count thing. It does not say anything of *a* tree; nor does it say anything of *trees;* nor does it say anything of a group of trees or of a part of a tree. In order for it to say anything of these sorts, it would have to read: "it's nice to have a tree" or "it's nice to have trees", and so on. It is only if (28) were expressed in one of these ways that it could be said to say something of a count thing or of count things. But then in that case it would not be saying something that has application *only* to a mass thing, so it still would not be a type crossing.

These same considerations can be applied to the following sequence:

(29) He found a gold in his yard.

It might be thought that (29) says of a mass thing something that has application only to a count thing. But this is not so. The expression 'a gold' does not designate any mass thing; therefore, (29) does not say anything of a mass thing. If (29) were expressed as "he found gold in his yard", then it *would* be saying something about a mass thing (namely, the substance gold), but in that case it would *not* be saying something that has application only to a count thing. So it would still not be a type crossing. In conclusion, then, I shall readily admit that (28) and (29) are ungrammatical, and, hence, that the class of nouns is not itself a grammatical class but needs to be divided into the subclasses of count nouns and mass nouns, which *are* true grammatical classes. However, given our working definition of 'type crossing', I shall have to deny that (28) and (29) are type crossings, for, despite the fact that they contain a count noun and a mass noun, respectively, they cannot be regarded as *saying something of* either a count thing or a mass thing. It seems as though our working definition of 'type crossing' precludes the possibility of formulating a type crossing based on this "count noun – mass noun" ungrammatically, which is, after all, more a matter of the presence or absence of an article ('a', 'the', etc.) or a plural ending than it is a matter of crossing types of thing. Therefore, still no good reason has been given for regarding type crossings as ungrammatical.

3.3. GRAMMATICALITY AND TRUTH

So far, I have mainly defended the negative thesis that there is no good reason to regard type crossings as ungrammatical. Now, in this section, I shall put forward a positive argument that type crossings definitely *are grammatical*. The argument is expressed in the following three premises and conclusion:

(1) The negations of type crossings are true statements.
(2) True statements are grammatical.
(3) Any sequence is grammatical if its negation is grammatical.
(4) Therefore, type crossings are grammatical.

The conclusion, (4), follows logically from the premises (1)–(3). So, if those premises are all true, then (4) must be true. Let us see, then, if (1)–(3) can be plausibly maintained.

Premise (1) is true on the basis of the argument presented earlier in Section 2.1. That argument is so persuasive. I cannot see how there is any more to be added to it.

Premise (2) is true, because if a sequence is ungrammatical, then it is senseless to inquire into its truth or falsity. Truth implies meaningfulness, and meaningfulness implies grammaticality, hence, truth must imply grammaticality. Another point is this: unless premise (2) is true, the whole appeal to grammar would be without purpose, for no one could then say that type crossings are meaningless because they are ungrammatical. On the contrary, we would then be inclined to say, "So what if type crossings are ungrammatical? They may still be meaningful and even express truths about the world", which is, of course, absurd. To avoid this absurdity, premise (2) must be regarded as true.

Premise (3) presents some technical difficulties. In particular, what could be meant by 'the negation of a sequence'? Suppose we say that the negation of a sequence is what results from placing the expression 'it is not the case that' in front of it. Then a counter-example could be brought up in the form of any question or command. If the expression 'it is not the case that' is placed before a question or command, the resulting sequence is ungrammatical. One way to avoid this difficulty is to break premise (3) down into the following two premises:

(3a) Any declarative sequence is grammatical if its negation is grammatical.

(3b) All type crossings are declarative sequences.

Since questions and commands are not declarative sequences, they are not counter-examples to (3a). But it is no easy matter to define this notion of a declarative sequence in a precise way. Presumably some appeal must be made to the idea of a sequence which "purports to be *stating* something", which is a rather imprecise idea. Nevertheless, I see no insuperable difficulties in all this. Once (3a) is clarified, it will be seen to be true, for the addition of the expression 'it is not the case that' to the beginning of any declarative sequence does not affect the grammaticality of the sequence.[15]

Philosophers and linguists generally accept the idea expressed

---

[15] Furthermore, it could plausibly be argued that the negation of any type crossing is capable of being formulated by placing the expression 'it is not the case that' in front of it. Consider, for example, "the theory is not blue" – "it is not the case that the theory is blue"; "he did not have a green thought" – "it is not the case that he had a green thought". Each member of the pair is equivalent to the other. Thus, the proposed definition of 'the negation of a sequence' is certainly applicable to the negations of type crossings.

in premise (3a). Since there are no clear counter-examples to it, I shall put it forward without further argument. Thus, inasmuch as (4) follows logically from premises (1)–(3b), all of which are true, it seems that (4) must be true as well. Hence, type crossings *are* grammatical.

3.4. TWO INTERMEDIATE POSITIONS

There are two ways to avoid saying that type crossings are either definitely grammatical or definitely ungrammatical. The first way is to maintain that the whole issue is a matter of arbitrary decision. And the second way is to maintain that it is all a matter of degree: type crossings are to a certain degree grammatical and to a certain degree ungrammatical. Let us consider these positions separately.

Two writers who maintain that the issue is a matter of arbitrary decision are Yehoshua Bar-Hillel and Michael Shorter. Bar-Hillel says the following:

> Whereas 'This stone is red', 'Aluminium is red', 'This stone weighs five pounds' are all meaningful sentences of ordinary English, 'Aluminium weighs five pounds' is not, and it does not matter in this connection whether we formulate this fact by saying that 'Aluminium weighs five pounds', though grammatically an impeccable sentence, is logically meaningless, or whether we prefer the more modern formulation that this word-sequence does not form a sentence at all.[16]

Shorter says the following:

> It is not grammatical rules that are fundamental but the meaningfulness or otherwise of forms of words. . . . Suppose for example that I formulate a set of rules and then find that the sentence 'virtue is

[16]   Yehoshua Bar-Hillel, "On Syntactical Categories", *Journal of Symbolic Logic*, XV (1950), p. 1. The example used here, "aluminium weighs five pounds", is a genuine type crossing. It does not, as might be thought, involve count noun – mass noun ungrammaticality, for it is more readily transformed into a clearly meaningful sentence by substitution of a proper name (or demonstrative noun phrase) for the mass noun 'aluminium' than by substitution of a count noun for it.

quickly' is in accordance with them. I shall then say, not that 'virtue is quickly' must be meaningful because it obeys the rules, but that the rules must be defective. I shall try to amend them accordingly. Similarly if I regard 'virtue is blue' as meaningless, I shall not be satisfied with a set of rules that admits it. If, therefore, one wants to support the claim that 'virtue is blue' is meaningful, it is no good appealing to a set of grammatical rules. An opponent can always produce a different set of rules and appeal to those. ... The rules themselves can at best be a systematic formulation of one's pre-existing ideas about meaning.[17]

I shall maintain that a position such as this is mistaken, for it entails the false view that there is no good reason to take type crossings to be grammatical. The results of Section 3.3 refute this view, and thus refute the position in question. To put it another way, there *is* an ordinary concept of grammar and it is sufficiently clear to warrant our judgement that type crossings are grammatical. For one thing, our ordinary concept of grammar does not warrant any grammatical distinctions among nouns, except possibly in the case of count nouns and mass nouns. And secondly, it *does* warrant the principles of grammaticality which were appealed to in the proof in Section 3.3, namely premises (2) and (3a). Thus, as far as our ordinary concept of grammar is concerned, type crossings *are* grammatical.

The second intermediate position, according to which type crossings are to a certain *degree* ungrammatical, is maintained by Noam Chomsky. He says the following:

Suppose we have a three-level hierarchy. Then C_1^1 is the class of all words. Let $C_1^2 =$ Nouns, $C_2^2 =$ Verbs, $C_3^2 =$ Adjectives, $C_4^2 =$ everything else. Let $C_1^3, \ldots, C_j^3$ be subcategories of Verbs (pure transitives, those with inanimate objects, etc.); subcategories of Nouns, and so on. Every sequence of words can now be represented by the sequence of first-level, second-level, third-level categories to which these words belong. Thus, "misery loves company" is represented $C_1^1 C_1^1 C_1^1$ on level one, $C_1^2 C_2^2 C_1^2$ (ie., NVN) on level two, $N_{abstr} V_{k}$-N_{abstr} on level three (where these are the appropriate C_i^3's). One of the selectional rules of the generative grammars (i.e., in the transforma-

17 Shorter, *op. cit.*, pp. 79-81.

tional model of [SS], one of the context-restricted constituent structure rules) will specify that V_k occurs only with animate subjects. Thus "misery loves company" will not be generated by the grammar, although "John loves company" will. However, "misery loves company" has a level two representation in common with a generated utterance, namely, NVN. We therefore call it semi-grammatical, on level two. "Abundant loves company", on the other hand, has only a level one representation in common with a generated utterance and is therefore labeled completely ungrammatical.

Without going into details, it is obvious how, in a similar way, a degree of grammaticalness can be assigned to any sequence of formatives when the generative grammar is supplemented by a hierarchy of categories. The degree of grammaticalness is a measure of the remoteness of an utterance from the generated set of perfectly well-formed sentences, and the common representing category sequence will indicate in what respects the utterance in question is deviant.[18]

The same objection that was applied to the first position can be applied to this one as well. Since type crossings have been shown to be grammatical, they cannot be to any degree ungrammatical. Thus, they cannot be, as Chomsky suggests, "semi-grammatical". To put it another way, the sentence structure of type crossings is the same as that of clearly meaningful sentences. But clearly meaningful sentences do not have the property of being "less grammatical than" anything else. Hence, type crossings could not have that property either.

Here is another objection: by virtue of Chomsky's theory, stated above, sentence (4) ("quadruplicity drinks procrastina-

---

[18]   Noam Chomsky, "Degrees of Grammaticalness", in *The Structure of Language,* ed. Jerry A. Fodor & Jerrold J. Katz (Englewood Cliffs, Prentice-Hall, Inc., 1964), p. 387. Paul Ziff is another writer who develops a notion of degree of grammaticality (*op. cit.,* pp. 209-210). But he is unclear about how it is to be applied to type crossings. Instead of saying "he had a green thought" is semi-grammatical (or to some *degree* ungrammatical), Ziff says simply that it *is ungrammatical.* He does not attempt to apply the notion of degree to it at all. – D. J. Hillman also mentions degree of grammaticality, but says that "it is a matter of choice whether we prefer a rigid distinction between sentences and non-sentences, or a graduated scale corresponding to our ability to grade utterances by their degree of acceptability" (*op. cit.,* p. 232).

tion") would *not* be less grammatical than sentence (27) ("a person's thoughts are in his brain"). Yet this seems counter-intuitive. If the notion of degree is to be at all applicable to type crossings, then we should expect a sentence like (4) to be less grammatical than a sentence like (27). As a reply to this criticism, it might be suggested that Chomsky's procedure could be pushed in the direction of distinguishing subclasses of concrete nouns and abstract nouns, and that on the basis of such distinctions (4) could be shown to be less grammatical than (27). But this leads to further difficulties. One such difficulty is that concrete-abstract type crossings would turn out to be less grammatical than intra-abstract type crossings, since the former involve a crossing of broader and more inclusive categories than do the latter. Yet this result is at variance with our intuitions on the matter. For example, we have no inclination at all to take the concrete-abstract type crossing "the theory of relativity is blue" to be less grammatical than the intra-abstract type crossing "moral perfection is a prime number". This shows, I think, that the division of nouns into subclasses (concrete nouns vs. abstract nouns, etc.) which is recommended by Chomsky and Ziff is purely *ad hoc* and even counter-intuitive. I would say, then, that although degree of grammaticality is a meaningful concept, the criterion for it must be purely intuitive and not capable of any precise exposition.

I hope to have shown that the two intermediate positions considered in this section are not applicable to type crossings (as restricted in 3.1). However, it may be that at least one of them does have application to a broader concept of type crossing. So, I shall put off further discussion of these positions to Chapter 8, where the "broader concept" will be introduced and critically examined.

3.5. PHILOSOPHY AND LINGUISTICS

I have thus far argued that, with respect to our ordinary concept of grammar, type crossings *are grammatical*. Therefore, they are neither ungrammatical nor semi-gammatical. But now suppose that they *were*, say, semi-grammatical. What would be the relevance of that to our earlier questions about type crossings? In what way would it provide answers to the following:

A) What are type crossings? (That is, what are the necessary and sufficient conditions for being a type crossing?)

B) How are type crossings to be distinguished from sentences (14)–(16)?

C) What is the ultimate basis of the meaninglessness of type crossings?

If Question A is interpreted in such a way that it does *not* include Question C, then I think that the appeal to grammar would go far in answering it, provided that type crossings are properly classified as semi-grammatical. Question A would then present a problem in theoretical linguistics rather than philosophy. This also holds for Question B. Presumably, those who maintain that type crossings are semi-grammatical would not go so far as to also classify (14)–(16) as semi-grammatical. They would no doubt acknowledge that although (14)–(16) are in many ways odd (perhaps even meaningless), this oddity is not of the grammatical sort. Therefore, the appeal to grammar (the subcategories of the class of nouns, etc.) *would* provide a way to distinguish type crossings from sentences such as (14)–(16), provided, again, that type crossings are to be considered semi-grammatical.

However, when it comes to Question C, it seems that the appeal to grammar will not in itself provide an answer, even given that type crossings are ungrammatical or semi-grammatical. The philosopher will want to press C by asking: what is the basis of those distinctions among subcategories of nouns which make type crossings at best semi-grammatical? Are those distinctions purely arbitrary or do they have some basis in either the way people speak in ordinary language or in the way people put concepts together in thought? Clearly, this is not a problem in linguistics, but a problem in philosophy (either philosophy of language or epistemology, or perhaps both). Therefore, although the appeal to grammar could be relevant to the linguistic problem of defining the concept of a type crossing and distinguishing type crossings from other sorts of sentences, it still does not provide an answer to our main philosophical problem of the basis of the meaninglessness of type crossing, even given that type crossings are ungrammatical or semi-grammatical.

Nevertheless, language may yet hold the key to this latter problem. It seems, then, that the way to go about the matter is to ask whether type crossings are meaningless (or false) because they violate rules of language, without specifying that these rules be considered grammatical rules. Advocates of this approach usually refer to such rules as "type-rules". Let us, therefore, proceed to explore this notion of a "type-rule".

TYPE-RULES

4.1. A LOOK AT THE LITERATURE

The first mention of type-rules was made by Gilbert Ryle in his article "Categories".[1] He says the following:

'Saturday is in bed' breaks no rule of grammar. Yet the sentence is absurd. . . .

When a sentence is (not true or false but) nonsensical or absurd, although its vocabulary is conventional and its grammatical construction is regular, we say that it is absurd because at least one ingredient expression in it is not of the right type to be coupled with or to be coupled in that way with the other ingredient expression or expressions in it. Such sentences, we may say, commit type-trespasses or break type-rules.

Although Ryle does not explain what he means by a "type-rule", he does offer what may be construed to be an example of one.[2] The rule reads:

(R): The dotted line in ". . . is false" can be completed with "What you are now saying . . ." and cannot be completed with "What I am now saying . . .".

The sentence which would break rule (R) is the following:

(S): What I am now saying is false.

The question arises whether (S) is really a type crossing. On this point, Ryle says the following:

---

[1] This first appeared in the *Proceedings of the Aristotelian Society*, XXXVIII (1937-38). The passage quoted is from pp. 194 and 200. The article is reprinted in *Logic and Language, Second Series,* edited by Antony Flew (Oxford, Blackwell, 1953); *cf.* pp. 70 and 75.

[2] *Ibid.,* p. 202. (Flew, p. 77.)

Latterly the attention of logicians has been focused on certain sorts of type-trespasses, like those which are committed by 'I am now lying' and " 'Heterological' is heterological". These sorts are interesting because their absurdities are not obvious but manifest themselves in the generation of contradictions or vicious circles, whereas 'Saturday is in bed' is obviously absurd before any contradictions are seen to result from the hypothesis that it is true.

Moreover we can be actually led by seemingly valid arguments to propounding propositions of the former sorts, whereas only the deliberate intention to produce balderdash would get us to formulate sentences of the latter sort. That is, some type-trespasses are insidious and others are not. It is the insidious ones which force us to consider type-rules; the others we only attend to because we are already considering type-rules. But it would be a mistake to restrict the theory of types to the theory of certain special type-rules.[3]

I gather from this passage that Ryle considers paradoxical sentences, such as those the construction of which was to be prevented by Bertrand Russell's theory of types, to be meaningless in the same way that type crossings are meaningless, the only difference being that the meaninglessness is readily apparent in the latter case but not in the former. Two other philosophers who hold this view are Bertrand Russell and Arthur Pap.[4]

The opposing view is expressed in a recent article by Fred Sommers.[5] He says the following:

Great damage has been done to the cause of linguistic clarity by placing the antinomies under "category mistakes" and considering a sentence like "I am a liar" to be the same sort of absurdity as "Wednesday is awake" only that in the latter case the absurdity is obvious while in the former case it has to be proven or exhibited.

What Sommers says here is quite right. This can be brought out if we consider the following two sentences:

(30) Sentence (30) is false.

---

[3] *Ibid.,* pp. 200-201. (Flew, pp. 75-76.) The article by A. J. Baker was written in opposition to Ryle's article. Note how the quotation on p. 26 above contradicts part of what Ryle says here.
[4] Russell, *op. cit.,* p. 174. Pap, *op. cit.,* pp. 41ff.
[5] Fred Sommers, "The Ordinary Language Tree", *Mind,* LXVII (1959), p. 182.

(31) My car is false.

It should be clear that the difference between (30) and (31) is something more than just the fact that one is not obviously absurd, while the other is. My car is not the *type of thing* that could be false. Sentence (30), on the other hand, *is* precisely the type of thing that could be false, namely, a sentence (or statement). Thus, (31) is a type crossing, whereas (30) is not. From (30) it is possible to derive unusual consequences (e.g., the consequence that (30) is not identical to "sentence (30) is false");[6] similarly, from what are called the "logical antinomies", as opposed to the "semantical antinomies", it is possible to derive consequences that are paradoxical in the strict logical sense. However, that is all that these sentences are – unusual, paradoxical. They do not involve type violations in the sense in which "the theory of relativity is blue" and sentence (31) involve type violations. They do not say of one type of thing something that has application only to another type of thing. They are therefore not type crossings.

Thus, where the term 'type-rule' is used in Ryle's sense, we cannot say that the meaninglessness of type crossings has its basis in the violation of type-rules. Hence, Ryle's notion of a type-rule just won't do for our purposes.

Another mention of type-rules is made by P. F. Strawson in his book *Introduction to Logical Theory*. After drawing several analogies between the formation rules of a logical system and the grammatical rules of ordinary language, Strawson says the following:

> ... we find that the grammatical requirements which are analogous to formation rules are not the only requirements a sentence must satisfy if it is to make sense. No grammatical rule is infringed by saying that the cube root of ten is three miles away or that there is a loud smell in the drawing-room. But to say either of these things would be, if not to talk nonsense, at least to say something which had no literal or straightforward sense. ...

---

[6] The proof for this sort of derivation is suggested in my article "The Paradox of the Non-Communicator", *Philosophical Studies*, XV (1964).

It seems, then, that there are additional requirements, besides those laxly imposed by grammar, on the ways in which words may be combined to make literal sense. We may refer to these as type-restrictions or type-rules; for they rule out combinations of expressions of certain types.[7]

Here again, the notion of a "type-rule" is mentioned but not satisfactorily explained. Strawson neither defines the term 'type-rule' nor clarifies it by means of examples. However, he does provide examples of type crossings, namely, "the cube root of ten is three miles away" and "there is a loud smell in the drawing-room". And he does seem to have the idea that the meaninglessness of type crossings has its basis in the violation of type-rules. Perhaps, then, we can construct the sort of rule he has in mind. For example, the type-rule violated by "the theory of relativity is blue" might be formulated as follows:

The only noun expressions which may be substituted for the 'x' in 'x is blue' (where 'blue' means the color blue) are those denoting spatially extended entities.

And the type-rule violated by "quadruplicity drinks procrastination" might be formulated as follows:

The only noun expressions which may be substituted for the 'x' and 'y' in 'x drinks y' (where 'drinks' is taken literally) are those denoting organisms with mouths, and liquids, respectively.[8]

I believe there would be great technical difficulties confronting the construction of a precise theory of type-rules, but I shall not go into those here. Rather, there is an important philosophical question that we must pursue, namely: what is the basis of the restrictions (or specifications) contained in type-rules? Are they restrictions which are in effect in ordinary language or are they merely *ad hoc* restrictions invented by philosophers to

---

[7] Strawson, *op. cit.*, pp. 226-227.

[8] I do not know whether Strawson would object to the terminology of these formulations or not. But in any case, such an objection would not be relevant to the present discussion, which approaches the problem only in the broadest possible terms.

define 'type crossing' or to aid in the construction of artificial languages? If type-rules are in effect in ordinary language,
then the basis of the restrictions contained in them is ordinary
linguistic practice or convention. On the other hand, if they are
merely *ad hoc* inventions, then the basis for those restrictions
must lie elsewhere, perhaps in something like the unthinkability
of type crossings or in our intuitions about types. This is a philo-
sophically large question, so let us proceed with care.

If type-rules are in effect in ordinary language, then presumably they would be implicit rules of the language, rather than
explicit rules, for no one has ever systematically formulated
them. Thus, the question of whether or not they are in effect in
ordinary language is not to be settled by appeal to books, but
by appeal to the linguistic behavior of ordinary speakers of the
language. I think the best criterion for settling this matter is
that of whether or not people have any tendency to correct themselves and others on the basis of type-rules. For presumably the
existence of implicit rules is derived from the practice of correcting on the basis of them. Where there is no practice of violation and correction, there is no sense in speaking of an implicit
rule.

Do people have any tendency to correct on the basis of type-
rules? To answer this, let us construct a hypothetical case. Suppose, in the course of a conversation, Jones says to Smith, "The
theory of relativity is blue". Would Smith have any tendency to
correct Jones on the basis of a type-rule? My answer is "No". I
do not think Smith would have any tendency to correct Jones on
the basis of a type-rule for two reasons, which I shall now proceed
to develop.

4.2. THE ARGUMENT FROM MISSING CONDITIONS

The first reason, which I shall call "the argument from missing
conditions", is as follows. In order for Smith to correct Jones on
the basis of a type-rule, two conditions must obtain. (1) Smith

must believe Jones to have made a linguistic mistake. Otherwise there would not be anything about Jones's utterance for him to correct. And (2), he must interpret Jones's utterance to be a type crossing. Otherwise, the relevant rule, on the basis of which correction is to be made, would not be a type-rule, but some other kind of rule. The argument, then, is that these two conditions never in fact arise. Smith would never believe Jones to have made a linguistic mistake and also to have uttered a type crossing. On the contrary, he would interpret the situation in any of a number of other ways.

For example, Smith might take Jones to have uttered a metaphor.[9] Or possibly he might take Jones's use of the expression 'the theory of relativity' to be an unusual or elliptical use, perhaps referring to a book or some other material object rather than to the theory of relativity itself (as was suggested on page 12). In this case, neither of the two conditions, mentioned above, would be fulfilled. Smith would not be interpreting Jones's utterance to be a linguistic mistake, nor would he be taking it as a type crossing. The situation here described is a very likely one because it involves people who know one another to be adequate speakers of the language – which is the most common conversational situation.

Another situation is that in which Smith is an adequate speaker of the language but Jones is not. Jones might be, say, a child or else a person whose native language is not English. In this situation, the first condition may very well obtain; that is, Smith may very well believe Jones to have made a linguistic mistake. But in that case I shall want to argue that Smith would *not* interpret Jones's utterance to be a type crossing. Rather, he would interpret it to be a vocabulary mistake. He might say, for example, "What you mean is that the theory of relativity is *true*, not that

[9] In order to do this, it is not necessary that Smith place some metaphorical interpretation on Jones's utterance. He may simply remark, "What you say is too profound for me" or something to that effect, in which case he would be taking Jones's utterance to be metaphorical, but such that he just does not get the metaphor.

it is blue." Here, Jones is being corrected on the basis of vocabulary, not on the basis of a type-rule. (And again, if Jones's utterance is the sentence "Saturday is in bed", Smith might correct him with the remark: "What you mean to say is that Saturday is to be spent in bed, not that it is in bed".) In the case of a person who has not as yet mastered his English, the linguistic mistake involved is not a type mistake, but *a failure to select the right words to express his thoughts.* Correction would therefore be made on the basis of vocabulary (or possibly grammar), not on the basis of a type-rule.

It may be objected that what has been said is not so in the case where fairly subtle "category mistakes" are concerned. Suppose, for example, that Jones is a confused philosopher who utters the sentence "a person's thoughts are in his brain". Here, so the objection goes, the two conditions might very well both obtain. Smith might very well believe Jones to have made a linguistic mistake and also interpret his utterance to be a type crossing. But what sort of linguistic mistake would Jones's utterance be? Is it not a vocabulary mistake? Jones must either be interpreting 'thoughts' to mean something like 'configurations of gray matter' or else be interpreting 'brain' to mean something like 'mind' or 'consciousness'. And both of these interpretations run counter to ordinary usage. Hence, if Jones utters the sentence "a person's thoughts are in his brain", it seems he must be making a vocabulary mistake, either with the word 'thoughts' or with the word 'brain'. So, even where comparatively subtle considerations are at stake, the linguistic mistake involved is not a type mistake, but a failure to select the right words to express one's thoughts. The proper reply to such a mistake would not be to cite a type-rule, but to cite a conventional definition.

The question may arise whether Jones could retract what he has said on the grounds that it expresses a type mistake (or "category mistake"). If Smith attacks his statement by pointing out that thoughts are not the type of thing that can be in a brain, could Jones come to agree with Smith and admit that he had been confused about types? Certainly Jones could retract his assertion and come to agree with Smith that thoughts are not the type of thing that could be in a brain. But the change in his position in this case would simply be that, whereas formerly he either used 'thoughts' to stand for something material or else used 'brain' to stand for something non-material, now he is using 'thoughts' and 'brain' in their conventional senses, where 'brain' stands for something material and 'thoughts' stands for something non-material. The mistake, then, is still a vocabulary mistake. The confusion is not a confusion about types, but a confusion about the conventional meanings of certain words. So, if type mistakes, by definition, involve confusion about types, then I must deny that such mistakes ever occur.

Of course, from a teacher's standpoint, it is useful to point out absurdities in the writing and speech of students by referring to those absurdities as, say, "category mistakes". But there is nothing of significance involved in this sort of mistake that is not also involved in cases of *factual* error due to linguistic confusion. For example, suppose a student intends to say that llamas are used as beasts of burden in Peru, but instead utters the sentence "*camels* are used as beasts of burden in Peru". He may know what a llama is in the sense that when he visualizes the sort of animal he wants to talk about, he visualizes a llama, not a camel. Yet he uses the wrong word to designate that animal. He thus makes a vocabulary mistake. But the resulting sentence is not a type crossing, but only a factually false statement. There is no essential difference between this case and the case of the "category mistake", for the essential point about them is that they are both mistakes in the use of some word or phrase. It is only a matter of chance that the sentence which embodies the mistake should turn out to be a type crossing rather than a factually false statement (or vice versa). For example, one who utters the type crossing "my thoughts are in my brain" might, instead, have expressed his confusion by uttering the sentence "the word 'thought' means 'configuration of gray matter' ", which is only factually false and not a type crossing. Hence, the fact that a type crossing is uttered, rather than a contingent falsehood, is of little significance. I conclude, then, that the teacher's comment, "This is a category mistake", is only an emphatic way of calling attention to the student's misuse of a certain word or phrase. The teacher could just as well have stated simply that the word or phrase is not conventionally used in the way in which the student has used it. This would have the same point, but probably less heuristic force.

It might be said, then, that the term "category mistake" is misleading, for it suggests that the mistake involved has to do with the nature of types or categories, so that the student needs information about the membership of such general classes. On the contrary, the sort of information required is not information about categories, but information about the conventional uses of words. Thus, correction of such a mistake might be made by appeal to a good dictionary, but not by appeal to type-rules. A category mistake, then, if it is to be said to sometimes occur, must be understood as only a special sort of vocabulary mistake – one which happens (by chance) to result in a type crossing rather than in some other sort of sentence.

To get back to Smith and Jones, it seems, then, that where Smith believes Jones to have made a linguistic mistake in his utterance "the theory of relativity is blue", he would not have any tendency to correct Jones on the basis of a type-rule, for he would see that Jones's problem is not that he is confused about types (and therefore needs information about types), but that the meaning he has assigned a given word runs counter to ordinary usage. Indeed, if Jones's utterance really were a genuine type crossing, then there would be no thoughts to express, for that which a type crossing purports to express is unthinkable. Thus, no one can ever *assert* a type crossing, for to assert something is to mean something by it. Since type crossings can have no meaning, they cannot be asserted. It follows that no sentence which expresses what a speaker really intends to assert could possibly be a type crossing (or involve type confusion).

We might well wonder, given the above discussion, whether the second condition could ever obtain. That is, are there any circumstances under which Smith would actually interpret Jones's utterance to be a type crossing? One circumstance, of course, is that in which Jones is using his utterance as an example, say, as an example of a meaningless sentence. The only other circumstance I can think of is that in which Jones utters the sentence, as Ryle puts it, with "the deliberate intention to produce balderdash". But in neither of these cases would Smith believe Jones to have made a linguistic mistake, or any kind of mistake for that matter. Thus, the first condition would not obtain. Hence, again, there would be no tendency whatsoever for Smith to correct Jones on the basis of a type-rule.

The conclusion of the argument from missing conditions is that type-rules are never used to correct anyone's linguistic performance because the conditions for such correction never in fact obtain. Hence, type-rules are not in effect in ordinary language. It might be mentioned, furthermore, that they are never taught or learned or cited or discussed. They are not written anywhere, nor are they passed on by word of mouth. No one but a handful of philosophers has ever even heard of them. As rules of ordinary language, they simply do not exist. It seems, then, that type-rules are at best only *ad hoc* philosophers' inventions.

4.3. THE ARGUMENT FROM NON-LINGUISTIC RESPONSE

My second reason for denying that language is subject to type-rules is what I shall call "the argument from non-linguistic response". So far, I have argued that the conditions for correction on the basis of a type-rule never in fact arise. But let us suppose they were to arise. That is, let us suppose that, after hearing Jones's utterance, "the theory of relativity is blue", Smith questions Jones and thereby learns that Jones's utterance: is not metaphorical, does not place any unusual or elliptical interpretation on the noun phrase 'the theory of relativity' or on the predicate 'is blue', is not a mistake in vocabulary or grammar, is not an example of anything, and is not supposed to be balderdash (i.e., Jones intends to be *asserting* it with all seriousness). Pre-

sumably, these are supposed to be the conditions under which
Smith would correct Jones on the basis of a type-rule.[10] The argument from non-linguistic response is that, given the conditions
described, Smith would *still* have no inclination whatsoever to
correct Jones on the basis of anything like a "rule of language".

Instead of correcting Jones, a much more plausible hypothesis
is that Smith would simply ask Jones what he means. Smith might
say, "I don't understand what you mean. Please explain." Or,
another response might be one in which Smith says: "You can't
say that. It's meaningless." But here again, Smith is not correcting
Jones; nor is he appealing to rules of language.

It may be objected at this point that although Smith is not
appealing explicitly to rules of language, nevertheless rules of
language are in some way behind his response that Jones's utterance is meaningless. To bring this out, suppose Jones were to
ask Smith: "Why can't I say it? Why is it meaningless?" In that
case, according to the objection, Smith should come out with a
direct appeal to a type-rule. He might say, for instance: "It's
meaningless because only spatially extended things can be said
to be blue."

The question now turns on this latter response, "Only spatially extended things can be said to be blue." Is this a rule of
language? It depends on what sort of grounds one is prepared

---

10   The form in which the type-rule is expressed need not, of course, be
the precise form suggested on page 61. It could be much more loosely
worded than that and still count as correction on the basis of a type-rule.
But even here there are limits. For example, Michael Shorter suggests
(*op. cit.*, p. 83ff.) that the negations of type crossings may themselves be
regarded as rules of language, thus, presumably, as type-rules. But I think
this is going too far. Despite the fact that the only use for the negations
of type crossings in ordinary discourse seems to be in teaching situations
(see page 24), it does not seem plausible to take these sentences as rules
of language. I cannot see, for example, how we could ever accept "the
theory of relativity is not blue" as a possible wording for the type-rule
violated by "the theory of relativity is blue". We just do not read the
negations of type crossings as rules. Furthermore, by the logical principle
of double negation, this approach would make type crossings themselves
the *negations of rules of language,* which is, of course, absurd. For these
reasons, I think Shorter's suggestion must be rejected.

to appeal to in order to support it. Suppose Jones were to press Smith still further with the question "Why can only spatially extended things be said to be blue?" Smith might plausibly reply, "Because it is *unthinkable* that something should have a color without having some sort of surface on which the color might go." However, to appeal to unthinkability is certainly not to appeal to linguistic conventions. If Smith were to appeal to such grounds as unthinkability, it would show clearly that his response "Only spatially extended things can be said to be blue" is *not* a rule of language, but a statement about the limits of thought or something of that sort. In order for Smith's response to be a rule of language, Smith would have to give as grounds for uttering it something other than the appeal to unthinkability mentioned above. He would have to say something like: "Only spatially extended things can be said to be blue because *that's the rule, that's English* (or that's the way language is)." But it seems to me highly unlikely that anything of this sort would be said. When I put myself in Smith's position, confronted by this queer utterance ("the theory of relativity is blue") under the conditions described above, I feel no inclination whatever to justify my response to Jones by saying "That's the rule" or "That's English" or anything of this sort. The reason a person rejects the sentence "the theory of relativity is blue" as meaningless (or odd) is not that the sentence violates rules about the use of the word 'blue'. After all, at no time in his life has anyone ever read or been told or come in contact with any such rules or conventions. Rather, the reason is that the person in a certain sense *sees* that color is a property of a surface, and surface requires spatial extension, and therefore only spatially extended things can be blue. When he says that only spatially extended things can *be said to* be blue, he is merely giving expression to this intuition about colors and surfaces; he is not appealing to any rule of ordinary language. My conclusion, then, is that since people have no tendency to correct on the basis of type-rules or anything resembling them, type-rules are not in effect in ordinary language.

It might be objected that type-rules are in effect in ordinary language in the same way that the rules of grammar are in effect. If Jones were to utter the sequence "the theory is but", Smith would not cite any rule to correct him. Yet surely it would be wrong to deny that Jones's utterance violates our rules of grammar.

In response to this objection, I must agree, first of all, that the sequence "the theory is but" does violate certain conventions of language which may be called "rules of grammar". I also agree that if Jones were to utter this queer sequence, Smith would probably not cite a rule in order to correct him, not even if the "conditions for correction", as described earlier, were to exist. However, Smith *would* make some reference to language. He might say, "That's not English (or that's bad English)" or something of the sort. At least some reference or appeal to *language* would be called-for. And it is precisely this fact which justifies our saying that Jones's utterance violates conventions of language. In other words, the criterion for whether or not a given sequence violates linguistic conventions is to see, in those cases where people balk at an utterance of the sequence, whether or not they refer or appeal to *language* in their reaction. The conclusion of the argument from non-linguistic response is not merely that Smith has no tendency to cite a type-rule when Jones utters the type-crossing "the theory of relativity is blue" under the specified conditions. Rather, it is that Smith has no tendency to make an appeal of any sort to language, English, or anything connected with linguistic rules or conventions.

In the book mentioned previously, Strawson says the following:

We do not judge our linguistic practice in the light of antecedently studied rules. We frame rules in the light of our study of our practice.[11]

My question is: what is the practice connected with type-rules? People do not correct one another on the basis of type-rules. Nor do schoolteachers or parents mention type-rules when teach-

---

[11] Strawson, *op. cit.*, p. 230.

ing the language to children. There seems to be no practice involved here at all. It is precisely on these grounds that I make my claim that type-rules are not in effect in ordinary language.

Suppose it is claimed that there *is* a practice connected with type crossings, namely, the practice of never uttering them. Clearly this will not do, for there are also an indefinite number of meaningful sentences which are never uttered.[12] Hence, no distinction would be drawn here between type crossings and meaningful sentences, let alone between type crossings and other sorts of meaningless sentence. These same remarks apply to any attempt to account for the meaninglessness of type crossings in terms of their "deviation from regularities" in ordinary speech.

Fred Sommers makes the statement: "All absurdity is the result of the violation of some rule".[13] If 'rule' is here meant to refer to a sentence having a certain form (e.g., the form 'so-and-so is not permitted'), then the statement is true, but uninteresting. All it would come to is the proposition that any absurd sentence can be construed to violate some rule, whether that rule be contrived or not. However, if 'rule' is meant to refer to rules which are actually in effect in ordinary language, then I hope to have shown that the statement is false, counter-examples being type crossings.

4.4. A RECAPITULATION

As in the case of grammar, there are two main problems con-

---

[12] Consider, for example, any completely contrived sentence such as the following: "Sir Archibald Granfy Gimbullsen dialed the number 304362958 and thereby got to speak to Miss Agnes Gogworthy". It is clear, I think, that there are far more meaningful sentences that never have been nor will be uttered than there are sentences, meaningful or not, that actually have been or will be uttered. Just think of the variety of ways in which the above sentence about Sir Archibald could be altered and still be meaningful. Mere alteration of the series of digits in the (telephone) number could produce a number of possibilities far greater than the total number of uttered sentences in human history.

[13] Sommers, *op. cit.,* p. 181,

nected with the appeal to type-rules, one a linguistic problem, the other a philosophical problem. The linguistic problem is that of defining type crossings and distinguishing them from other kinds of sentences. The philosophical problem is that of explaining the ultimate basis of the meaninglessness of type crossings. It is the philosophical problem with which we have been concerned in this chapter. I hope to have shown that there is no point in saying of type crossings that they are meaningless *because* they violate type-rules, for such an explanation is completely *ad hoc*. Type-rules are not in effect in ordinary language. They are merely constructs invented by philosophers to facilitate discussion of type crossings and possibly to serve as formation rules of artificial languages.

But let us suppose that type-rules were in effect in ordinary language. What would be the philosophical significance of that? I would still argue that they do not provide any adequate explanation for the meaninglessness of type crossings, for the question would still arise: what is the basis of these type-rules? Is it that people just *arbritrarily agree* to use words in the way specified by the type-rules? Or is it that they *have to* use words in that way in order for their sentences to express combinations of concepts which can be grasped by the mind? In the latter case, to violate a type-rule is *not* to say something which goes against a man-made convention; rather, it is to say something which simply could not be thought. I think this latter alternative is the correct one. Although it is a matter of convention that we spell words in a certain way and it is a matter of convention that we use certain symbols for the purposes of punctuation, it is *not* a matter of convention that a particular sentence, given a certain interpretation for individual words in it, should or should not be a type crossing. That theories cannot intelligibly be said to be blue seems not to be a result of human design. I conclude, therefore, that the problem of explaining the meaninglessness of type crossings cannot be solved by appeal to the notion of rules of language, whether they be grammatical rules or any other kind of rules. Nor can it be solved by appeal to linguistic conventions or linguistic regularities. Language simply does not hold the key to this philosophical problem. Thus, we shall eventually have to look elsewhere for a solution to it. This will be done in later chapters.

Let us now consider briefly the linguistic problem. Is there any chance that the appeal to type-rules could provide a way of defining type crossings and distinguishing them from other kinds of sentences, such as sentences (14)–(16)? It seems not, for such a definition must ultimately be circular. Since type-rules are not in effect in ordinary language, they are not something we have before us to be discovered and investigated. Rather, they are *invented* by the same process that goes into the formulation of type crossings themselves. Thus, we could just as well define 'type-rules' as 'that which type crossings violate'. Then to say "S is a type crossing since it violates type-rules" is to say no more than "S is a type crossing since it violates what type crossings violate", which is to say nothing. There can be no evidence that S violates type-rules apart from the evidence that it is a type crossing. Therefore no new light is thrown on type crossings by defining them as 'sentences which violate type-rules' or in any similar way. Such a definition could have neither point nor purpose, since it must ultimately be circular. It seems, then, that even with respect to our linguistic problem, we shall have to look elsewhere for a solution.

5

TWO THEORIES OF TYPE CROSSINGS

5.1. GILBERT RYLE'S THEORY

Our linguistic problem is that of defining type crossings and distinguishing them from other kinds of sentences, especially from (14)–(16). I shall pursue this problem further both in the present chapter and in Chapter 6.

In the previous chapter it was suggested that Ryle's approach to type crossings is the "type-rule theory". However, taking another look at his article "Categories", I would like to suggest now that perhaps that is not so. On the contrary, Ryle seems to have our concept of a type crossing as a sentence which says of one type of thing something that has application only to a different type of thing.[1] Although this is the concept with which we have thus far been working, it is not a precise concept, for the question naturally arises: what is the criterion for 'different type'? Ryle provides such a criterion in the following terms:

Two proposition-factors are of different categories or types, if there are sentence-frames such that when the expressions for those factors are imported as alternative complements to the same gap-signs, the resultant sentences are significant in the one case and absurd in the other.[2]

I shall take this attempt to clarify the expression 'different type' as "Ryle's theory of type crossings", for it provides what is essentially lacking in our working definition of a type cross-

[1] Ryle expresses this concept in his characterization of a type crossing as a sentence which "is absurd because at least one ingredient expression in it is not of the right type to be coupled with or to be coupled in that way with the other ingredient expression or expressions in it". See the first quotation on page 58, above.
[2] Ryle, op. cit., p. 203. (Flew, pp. 77-78.)

ing.[3] The application of Ryle's criterion can be illustrated by the fact that the theory of relativity and, say, the sky over Ithaca turn out to be different types of thing, since the result of substituting 'the sky over Ithaca' for the gap-sign in "—— is blue" is a meaningful sentence, whereas the result of substituting 'the theory of relativity' for that gap-sign is a meaningless sentence.

One objection to Ryle's criterion, stated by J. J. C. Smart,[4] is as follows:

It is worthwhile to consider whether this test, if pushed to the limit, may not show every expression to be a different logical category from every other. (In which case we should be wise not to take it too seriously.) Thus, 'the seat of the —— is hard' works if 'chair' or 'bench' is put into the blank, but not if 'table' or 'bed' is. And if furniture words do not form a category, we may well ask what do.

Smart is here arguing that the sentence "the seat of the chair is hard" is meaningful, but the sentence "the seat of the bed is hard" is meaningless. Therefore, the nouns 'chair' and 'bed' turn out to be of different types. This is an unacceptable consequence, according to Smart, because it leads to the conclusion that every expression is of a different type from every other.

However, it is doubtful that this conclusion really follows. All that follows, it seems, is that there are a great many more types than philosophers formerly believed. Ryle accepts and defends this latter conclusion in terms of various expressions from the game of Bridge. He says the following:

The truth is that there are not just two or just ten different logical *métiers* open to the terms or concepts we employ in ordinary or technical discourse, there are indefinitely many such different *métiers* and indefinitely many dimensions of these differences.

I adduced the six Bridge terms, 'singleton', 'trump', 'vulnerable',

[3] One slight change needs to be made, however. The term 'proposition-factors' needs to be replaced by the term 'things', so as to restrict the theory to type crossings in the narrow sense, as defined in Section 3.1. If the theory is found not to work for type crossings in the narrow sense, then it must be considered inadequate for type crossings in the broad sense as well.

[4] J. J. C. Smart, "A Note on Categories", *The British Journal for the Philosophy of Sicence,* IV (1953), pp. 227-228.

'slam', 'finesse', and 'revoke', as terms none of which will go into
any one of Aristotle's ten pigeon-holes. But now we should notice
as well, that though all alike belong to the specialist lingo of a
single card-game, not one of them is, in an enlarged sense of 'category', of the same category with any of the other five. We can ask
whether a card is a diamond or a spade or a club or a heart; but
not whether a card is a singleton or a trump; not whether a game
ended in a slam or in a revoke; not whether a pair of players is
vulnerable or a finesse. None of the terms is a co-member of an
either-or set with any of the others. The same thing is true of most
though naturally not all of the terms that one might pick at random
out of the glossaries of financiers, ecologists, surgeons, garage-
mechanics and legislators.[5]

Ryle's conception of types is the rather loose notion of classes of
terms which will fit into various logical forms. He says:

In fact the distinction between the logical types of ideas is identical
with the discrimination between the logical forms of propositions
from which the ideas are abstractions. If one proposition has factors
of different types from those of another proposition, those propositions are different logical forms and have different sorts of logical
powers. The rules governing the conjunctions of propositions in valid
arguments reflect the logical constitutions of their various abstrac-
tible factors and features. There are as many types of terms as there
are forms of propositions, just as there are as many uphill as down-
hill slopes.[6]

Given this view of types, the fact that different furniture words
are of different types does not seem to be any objection at all.
Nor does it follow that every expression is of a different type
from every other.

There are at least two objections, however, which, I think, do
constitute a refutation of Ryle's theory. The first objection is that
the criterion for 'different type' is stated in terms of the
existence of sentence-frames of a certain sort. It seems, then,
that in order to show that two things are *not* of different types,

<hr />

[5]   Gilbert Ryle, *Dilemmas* (Cambridge, Cambridge University Press, 1954),
pp. 10-11.
[6]   Gilbert Ryle, *Philosophical Arguments* (Oxford University Press, 1945),
p. 9.

one must show that there do *not* exist sentence-frames of the required sort. But since there is no contradiction in the supposition that such sentence-frames exist, it would not be possible to show that. In order to demonstrate that sentence-frames of the required sort do not exist, one would have to complete an infinite series of tests, which is impossible. It follows that Ryle's theory could never be used to show of any sentence that it is *not* a type crossing, except perhaps in the case of a clearly meaningful sentence. This, I think, is a serious handicap, for there are many sentences which are neither clearly meaningful nor type crossings. With respect to such sentences, Ryle's theory provides no basis for classification.

If we add the proviso that type crossings are meaningless, then Ryle's theory would be essentially the same as the condition put forward in Section 3.1 (page 40). It could thus be expressed as follows:

A type crossing is a meaningless sentence which is capable of being transformed into a clearly meaningful sentence by substituting for at least one of the noun morphemes or regular noun phrases in it a different noun morpheme or regular noun phrase.

If Smart's example, "the seat of the bed is hard", is regarded as meaningless, then it would turn out to be a type crossing by virtue of the above definition. I have no objection to this. However, certain other examples where the noun morpheme plays a minor grammatical role in the sequence do not work so well. For example, consider the following sequence, taken from D. J. Hillman:[7]

(32) I went to the cinema this John.

This sequence does fit the above definition of 'type crossing', as can be seen by substituting, say, 'Saturday' for 'John'. But it does not fit our working definition of a type crossing, for it cannot be construed as *saying something of* John (or *of* a person). This shows that although the revised version of Ryle's theory is similar

---

[7] Hillman, *op. cit.*, p. 230.

to the original in basic features, there are also certain respects in which it is different. And these are brought out by isolated examples such as (32), which turn out to be type crossings on the revised version but not on the original version. Nevertheless, as long as we stay clear of such examples, there is no good reason why Ryle's theory cannot be expressed by this new version. Expressing it in this way does make it more workable as a criterion for 'being a type crossing'. But whichever version is used to express it, the theory is still open to the first objection, stated above.

The question arises whether sentences (14)–(16) turn out to be type crossings on Ryle's theory. It can be seen that by substitution of one noun morpheme or regular noun phrase for another, (14)–(16) *can* each be transformed into a clearly meaningful sentence. For example, by substituting 'green things' for 'red things', (14) is transformed into "some green things are all green" which is clearly meaningful. By substituting 'simultaneity' for 'precedence', (15) is transformed into "temporal simultaneity is a symmetrical relation" which is clearly meaningful. And finally, by substituting 'two adjacent edges' for 'three adjacent edges', (16) is likewise transformed into a clearly meaningful sentence. It follows that whether or not (14)–(16) are type crossings by virtue of Ryle's theory depends on whether or not they are to be regarded as meaningless. And this is true no matter which version of the theory we care to work with. But whether or not (14)–(16) are to be regarded as meaningless is not clear. Certainly they are not meaningless in exactly the same way that type crossings are meaningless. Yet, as in the case of type crossings, we cannot understand what it would be like for them to be true. What is needed, then, in order to decide the matter is some criterion of meaninglessness.

This brings me to the second objection to Ryle's theory, which is simply that no criterion of meaninglessness is provided. Ryle himself felt this difficulty, as he ended his article with the question: "But what are the tests of absurdity?" Ryle's theory rests heavily on the concept of meaninglessness. Therefore, unless a criterion for that concept is provided, the theory will have to be regarded as too obscure to be of any use.

Hillman attempts to revise Ryle's theory so as to avoid this obscurity. He says the following:

> the sentence "Saturday is in bed" is a *deviant utterance*. Looking at the matter in this way, we no longer say that the sentence is absurd on the basis of its infraction of some pre-analytic allocation of words to categories, but only that it deviates in some way from the stand-ard uses of sentences containing the word 'Saturday', which our C3 has already allowed us to describe in partial terms. Changing our perspective in this way, we once again eliminate reference to the troublesome concept of absurdity, which has resisted, and continues to resist, clarification.[8]

Hillman's criterion C3, which is supposed to partly clarify what is meant by a "deviant utterance", is stated as follows:

> C3 If A is an English expression, and E and E' environments of English, then (the occurrence of) A in E is assigned to a cate-gory different from that to which (the occurrence of) A in E' is assigned if:
> (1) E complemented by A is a sentence
> (2) E' complemented by A is a sentence
> (3) There exists an A', such that E complemented by A' is a sentence, whereas E' complemented by A' is a non-sentence.[9]

Thus, "Saturday is in bed" is a deviant sentence because there is an English expression, namely 'John', which, when put in place of 'Saturday', converts that sentence into another sentence, but which converts the alternative sentence "I went to the cinema this Saturday" into a non-sentence.

This criterion is so complicated that it is self-defeating. Even if we are given a clear-cut way of distinguishing sentences from non-sentences (which we aren't), I still see no way to show of our *other* examples of type crossings that they are deviant on the basis of this criterion. Consider, for example, "the theory of relativity is blue". In order to show that this sentence is

[8] *Ibid.,* **p.** 234.
[9] *Ibid.,* **p.** 233.

deviant we must be able to find an English expression, A', such that "A' is blue" is a sentence, and also find a sentence, E', containing the expression 'the theory of relativity', such that the result of substituting A' for 'the theory of relativity' in E' is a non-sentence. After working at this for a considerable time, I still have not been able to come up with any expression and sentence which will work. In fact, I cannot find any type crossing at all, other than the particular one Hillman uses ("Saturday is in bed"), which can be shown to be deviant on the basis of Hillman's criterion. Maybe I have not looked hard enough. On the other hand, the criterion imposes so many abstruse requirements that it seems extremely doubtful that *every* possible type crossing will be capable of being shown to be deviant on the basis of it. For this reason, Hillman's alternative to Ryle's theory of type crossings is even worse off than the original, for it is not even workable.

My conclusion to this section is that Ryle's theory is too obscure to constitute an adequate definition of 'type crossing', and also too obscure to permit the necessary distinction to be drawn between type crossings and sentences (14)–(16). And since Hillman's proposed revision of the theory has proved to be unworkable, it seems that we will have to search elsewhere for a basis on which to construct a theory of type crossings. I turn now to a radically different approach to the problem.

5.2. ARTHUR PAP'S THEORY

Although Arthur Pap never addressed himself to the problem of defining the notion of a type crossing, it is possible to construct a theory of type crossings from various remarks which he makes in the article "Types and Meaninglessness".[10] At the very end of that article, he says:

[10] The article in *Mind,* published shortly after Pap's death, is an adaptation of a paper, bearing the same title, which was read before the American Philosophical Association, Eastern Division, in December 1957 as part of a symposium with Max Black.

The locution "x is not the sort of thing to which predicate P can be ascribed", which is frequently used by ordinary-language-analysts who caution against category mistakes, expresses nothing else than the feeling that "x is P" is meaningless, or unlimitedly false, because a presupposed type predication is false.

This passage suggests the following definition:

D1: A type crossing is a sentence which presupposes a false type predication.

The definitions for 'presupposes' and 'type predication' are suggested earlier [11] in the article. They are as follows:

D2: 'S presupposes T' means 'the falsity of T entails the meaninglessness of S'.
D3: 'T is a type predication' means 'T can be transposed into a sentence of the form 'xεa', where a is a type'.

For Pap, the word 'type', as it appears here, is a technical term whose meaning he explains as follows:

A type is a class such that there are families of predicates which can be significantly, i.e. correctly or falsely, ascribed to all and only members of it. A predicate family is a set of predicates such that one and only one member of it must be true of anything of which some member of the set is true or false. Simple sounds constitute a type relative to pitch predicates, smallest visible spots relative to colour predicates, propositions relative to truth-value predicates but also relative to predicates designating cognitive attitudes (like "is believed by A at time t", "is disbelieved by A at time t", etc.), integers relative to odd and even, arguments relative to valid and invalid, and so on.[12]

Pap gives the following examples of type predications:

True type predications	False type predications
Socrates is a person.	Socrates is a number.
Modesty is a form of behaviour.	Modesty is something that has shape.
Molecules are postulated scientific objects.	Molecules are perceptual objects.

[11] *Ibid.*, pp. 47-48.
[12] *Ibid.*, p. 48.

Thoughts are mental events.   Thoughts are physical events in
                                   physical space.[13]

Pap's examples of sentences which presuppose the false type
predications listed above, respectively (and which are therefore
type crossings), are the following:

Socrates is a prime number.
Modesty is triangular.
Molecules are hot.
My thoughts are in my brain.

The predicates of these four type crossings might be called "type
ascribed predicates" because each of them can be meaningfully
ascribed to all and only members of some type. The predicate
'is a prime number' can be meaningfully ascribed to all and only
numbers, the predicate 'is triangular' can be meaningfully ascribed
to all and only things having some shape, and so on. Pap calls the
predicates which express types "type predicates". Thus, 'is a
number', 'is something having a shape', etc. are type predicates.

The relationship between type ascribed predicates and their
corresponding type predicates is twofold. It is, first of all, a
species-genus relation. For example, prime numbers could be
called a species of number, triangular things could be called a
species of thing having shape, and so on. Second, and more im-
portantly, type predicates express the range of significance of
their corresponding type ascribed predicates. Thus, all and only
numbers can be significantly called "prime numbers", all and
only things having shape can be significantly called "triangular",
and so on. In the case of our example "the theory of relativity is
blue" the type ascribed predicate is 'is blue' and the type predicate is 'is a spatially extended entity'. Thus, the sentence "the
theory of relativity is blue" is a type crossing, on Pap's view,
because it presupposes the false type predication "the theory of
relativity is a spatially extended entity".

This theory of type crossings seems to provide a basis for dis-

---

[13] *Ibid.*, p. 54. These examples are suggested, but not given in exactly the
same form in which they are stated here.

tinguishing type crossings from other non-definitional a priori falsehoods, such as (14)–(16), for, admittedly, there are no false type predications presupposed by "some red things are all green", "temporal precedence is a symmetrical relation", etc. So, from this point of view the theory seems satisfactory. But can it be used to test of given sentences whether or not they are type crossings? Let us consider this question.

If they are put together to form a criterion for type crossings, definitions D1, D2, and D3 would read as follows:

A sentence S is a type crossing if and only if there exists a sentence, T, which meets the following requirements:
  (1) T is false
  (2) The falsity of T entails the meaninglessness of S
  (3) T can be transposed into a sentence of the form 'xεα', where α is a type (as defined by Pap).

It seems to me that there are at least two difficulties with this criterion. First, there is the problem of its existential form. Since it is stated in terms of the *existence* of a sentence having certain properties, it seems, by virtue of the same reasoning as was suggested with regard to Ryle's theory, that no sentence could ever be demonstrated by it to be *not* a type crossing. It could not be shown, for example, with respect to the sentence "some red things are all green", that there does not exist a sentence, T, meeting the three requirements. The usefulness of the criterion is therefore severely limited.

The second difficulty has to do with the obscurity surrounding requirement (3). How can it be determined of a sentence that it is or is not a type predication unless there is given a list of all possible type predications? Or, as Max Black has put it, "it seems that in order to determine whether a given class is a type, in Mr. Pap's sense, we must have at our disposal a prior inventory of types".[14] The reason for this is that Pap's definition

---

[14] Max Black, "Comments on Arthur Pap's 'Types and Meaninglessness' ", paper read before the American Philosophical Association, Eastern Division, December 1957, as part of a symposium with Arthur Pap.

of 'type' does not provide any workable criterion for determining whether or not a given class is a type. For one thing, like the definition of 'type crossing' itself, it suffers from the difficulty about existential form. There would be no way to apply it so as to demonstrate that a given class is *not* a type. For another thing, it is not even clear how one should go about proving that a given class *is* a type. This obscurity is due partly to the complexity of the criterion and partly to the fact that, like Ryle's theory, it appeals to the concept of meaninglessness without defining that concept. (Such an appeal is made in requirement (2) as well as in requirement (3).) Since meaninglessness is a notoriously obscure and ambiguous notion, any theory making use of it needs to specify some test whereby sentences can be determined to be meaningless or not meaningless.[15]

Although Pap does not specify such a test, he did at one time [16] suggest a theory of cognitive significance applicable to type crossings. This is what he said:

... it may be suggested that *some* questions of cognitive significance, at any rate, can be decided only by intuition, and that considerations of possibilities of empirical testing seem rather extraneous to them. If we reject, e.g., "the number Two is blue" as meaningless rather than false, whereas we reject "the number Two is not a prime number" as false, it is not because the former sentence, and not the latter, is empirically unverifiable: empirical tests are as irrelevant to the one as to the other. It is just that we intuit that colors are significantly predicable only of spatially extended entities. Similarly, by just grasping the meanings of 'nation' and 'square', we see that the conjunction of these concepts is not significantly predicable of anything, and on this ground reject a sentence like "the French nation is square" as meaningless. On the basis of such intuitions we

[15]   Another objection is the fact that no clear distinction is drawn between a type, as in the concept of a *type* crossing, and a type, as in the expression 'Russell's theory of *types*'. On this point, see the review of Pap's "Types and Meaninglessness" by R. O. Gandy in *The Journal of Symbolic Logic*, XXV (1960), pp. 333-334.

[16]   This appears in a set of unpublished mimeographed pages which Pap distributed among his graduate students at Yale University. (I was one of those students in 1955-56.) The pages bear the title "Supplements and Revisions; *Elements of Analytic Philosophy,* Chapter 13".

may indeed construct the empiricist language in such a way that the sequence of words "the French nation is square", as well as "the number Two is blue", would not even be a sentence in it.** But it would obviously be putting the cart before the horse to say that these sentences of ordinary English with its imperfect syntactic rules are meaningless *because* they are not translatable into the preferred ideal language.

** It would be a spurious evasion of the appeal to intuition if one were to say "the number Two is blue" is not a sentence of the language with ideal syntax because 'the number Two' does not have the *type* required for substitutability in "x is blue", whereas 'the sky', 'the book on the table', etc. do have the right type. For to determine whether two expressions have the same or different type is to determine whether anything is significantly predicable of both the entities denoted by one and the entities denoted by the other. Thus we have to return to the intuitive test of significance anyway.

I think there is much to be said for the view that the only way to determine whether a sentence is a type crossing is by appeal to some intuitive test of significance, and I shall take this matter up in Chapters 6 and 7. Nevertheless, without further clarification of what is meant by "intuition", Pap's theory is certainly open to the charge of incompleteness, if not obscurity.

I shall now turn to a more basic difficulty pervading Pap's theory, one which it will be worthwhile to examine in some detail. The difficulty has to do with the fact that in Pap's theory type predicates have an unlimited range of significance and therefore cannot themselves be type ascribed predicates. In other words, type predications (sentences of the form 'S is P', where P is a type predicate) do not themselves presuppose false type predications. According to Pap's theory, then, the following sentences are *not* type crossings:

Socrates is a proposition.
Africa is an event.
My left ear is an attribute.

Pap has to maintain that these sentences, along with all other type predications, whether true or false, are actually meaningful sentences.

One difficulty in this view is pointed out by Max Black.[17] Ac-

17 In the APA paper mentioned above.

cording to Black, a predicate such as 'is a logician' would turn out to be a type predicate on Pap's view, because it designates the range of significance of the complex (type ascribed) predicate 'is admired by every other logician'. That is, "x is admired by every other logician" presupposes that x is a logician. Therefore, the class of logicians is a type, and 'is a logician' is a type predicate. In this fashion, just about any predicate at all could be shown to be a type predicate, including predicates such as 'is a prime number'. It follows that sentences such as "virtue is a logician" and "Socrates is a prime number" are actually type predications, on Pap's view, and must be taken to be meaningful.

Pap attempted to avoid this difficulty in his article, but without much success.[18] Nevertheless, he could have avoided it had he

---

[18] Pap says the following: "Professor Max Black called my attention to the fact that by admitting predicates of the form "has relation R to every *other* member of K" (e.g., "is admired by every other logician") one can obtain curious types on my definition. Thus, "is admired by every other logician" is true or false of logicians only, since any significant application of this predicate presupposes that the subject is a logician; hence the class of all logicians becomes a type! But let us analyze what we *assert* about x in saying "x is admired by every other logician": for every y, if y is a logician and y is different from x, then y admires x (that x is himself a logician is presupposed rather than asserted). It then appears that the range of values of x extends far beyond the class of logicians" (*op. cit.,* p. 50).

Pap apparently believes here that since the range of values of x in 'y admires x' extends beyond the class of logicians, the predicate 'is admired by every other logician' is not true or false only of logicians. But this is a blunder, for he admits that 'x is admired by every other logician' presupposes 'x is a logician'; and in his sense of 'presupposes' this constitutes an admission that the predicate 'is admired by every other logician' is significantly applicable (hence true or false) only of logicians. In order for the predicate in question to be significantly applicable to non-logicians, *two* necessary conditions must be fulfilled: (1) the range of values of x in 'y admires x' must extend beyond the class of logicians; (2) 'x is admired by every other logician' must *not* presuppose 'x is a logician'. Neither of these is a sufficient condition. (Pap's error apparently lay in thinking that (1) is a sufficient condition as well as a necessary condition.) Since condition (2) is unfulfilled, the predicate in question is not significantly applicable to non-logicians. It follows that, by virtue of such a predicate, the class of logicians becomes a type and 'is a logician' becomes a type predicate. Thus, it turns out, according to Pap's theory, that the sentence "the theory of relativity is a logician" is perfectly meaningful.

defined 'types' as 'ranges of significance of *syntactically simple* predicates' and then constructed a definition of 'syntactically simple' which would exclude predicates of the form 'bears relation R to every other member of class K'. By introducing this restriction into the definition of 'type', the predicate 'is a logician' would not be a type predicate even though it designates the range of significance of 'is admired by every other logician', for the latter predicate is not syntactically simple.

Pap's view that type predicates have an unlimited range of significance was expressed in opposition to the earlier view, maintained by Bertrand Russell and Rudolph Carnap, that type predicates designate their own range of significance. Russell says the following:

The characteristic of a type is that if t is a type, we have (x). xεt, and conversely, if (x).xεt, then t is a type. For in that case "xεt" is true whenever it is significant, i.e. whenever x belongs to the type which is the range of significance of x in "xεt". Consequently t is this range of significance, i.e. is a type.[19]

Carnap says the following:

In the word-series 'dog', 'animal', 'living creature', 'thing', every word is a more comprehensive predicate than the previous one, but only the last is a universal predicate. In the corresponding series of sentences 'Caro is a dog', '. . . is an animal', '. . . a living creature', 'Caro is a thing', the content is successively diminished. But the final sentence is fundamentally different from the preceding ones, in that its L-content is null and it is analytic. If in 'Caro is a thing', 'Caro' is replaced by any other thing-designation, the result is again an analytic sentence; but if 'Caro' is replaced by an expression which is not a thing-designation, the result is not a sentence at all.[20]

I gather from these passages that both Russell and Carnap take the range of significance of a type predicate (Carnap calls it a

---

[19] Whitehead and Russell, *Principia Mathematica*, Volume I (Cambridge University Press, 1957 edition), p. 400. I assume Russell is the author of the passage, since his name is usually associated with the theory of types stated in the book.

[20] Rudolph Carnap, *The Logical Syntax of Language* (New York, The Humanities Press, Inc., 1937), p. 293.

"universal predicate") to be the same as its truth range, in which case a type predicate may be said to designate its own range of significance. Thus, the range of significance of the type predicate 'is a spatially extended thing' is the class of spatially extended things, and the range of significance of the type predicate 'is a number' is the class of numbers. In other words, a type predication is true if and only if it is meaningful. Both Russell and Carnap would take the sentences "the theory of relativity is a spatially extended thing" and "Socrates is a number" to be meaningless. Presumably, such sentences are properly classified as type crossings.

In taking the opposing view, Pap would say of the two sentences mentioned that they, as well as all other type predications, are not meaningless; it is simply false that Socrates is a number, etc. For Pap, the range of significance of a type predicate is unlimited; so it can be meaningfully applied to any subject at all. He tries to justify this in the following way:

> If I deny that my thoughts are in my brain, I am likely to be challenged to specify their true location, though my intent was to deny that thoughts have any spatial location at all. If I deny that the molecules of which the air is composed are themselves hot, I might be taken to mean that they are cold, or lukewarm, or cool. In the case of a type predication, on the other hand, "not-(S is P)" is equivalent to "S is non-P", and for this reason a denial of "Socrates is a number" is intuitively more plausible than a denial of, say, "Socrates is divisible by an even square number". Having denied a type predicate P to an entity, I can go on and ascribe a type predicate incompatible with P to it: Socrates is not a number, but a person; modesty is not something that has shape, but a form of behaviour; molecules are not perceptual objects, but postulated scientific objects; thoughts are not physical events in physical space, but mental events.[21]

It does not seem to me that Pap has successfully defended his view, for I do not see that he has shown type predicates to have any special property not possessed by other predicates. It is true that we can say, "Socrates is not a number, but a person", and

[21]   Pap, *op. cit.*, p. 54.

so on, but we can also say, "Socrates is not a science, but a person" or "Socrates is not a chair, but a person" and still be speaking intelligibly. Yet, in these latter cases, the predicate denied to Socrates is *not* a type predicate. In a certain sense, it is true that a denial of "Socrates is a number" is more plausible than a denial of "Socrates is divisible by an even square number". But the reason for this has nothing to do with the fact that 'is a number' is a type predicate. The predicate 'is a chair' is not a type predicate, yet a denial of "Socrates is a number" is not more plausible than a denial of "Socrates is a chair". The reason why "Socrates is not divisible by an even square number" is less plausible than both "Socrates is not a number" and "Socrates is not a chair" is that, whereas someone (say, a child or foreigner) could conceivably need correction of some vocabulary mistake by means of one of the latter sentences, this does not seem possible with respect to the former sentence. We can easily imagine a case in which someone who does not know the language well could be misled into thinking that Socrates is some kind of thing other than a person, whether that kind of thing be a "type" in the strict sense (e.g., numbers, propositions, simple sounds) or whether it be some class other than a type (e.g., chairs, elephants, peanuts). But we cannot easily imagine a case in which someone could come to believe that something is divisible by an even square number without making the calculation involved (i.e., dividing by an even square number). And it is implausible, to say the least, that anyone should make such a calculation on Socrates. To put it another way, the reason why "Socrates is not a number" is more plausible than "Socrates is not divisible by an even square number" is that the former, unlike the latter, could conceivably have some *use* in ordinary discourse.

False type predications fit our working definition of a "type crossing". That is, they can be taken to say of one type of thing something that has application only to a different type of thing. Therefore, we must take them to be type crossings. And since false type predications, like other type crossings, express a combination of concepts that is literally unthinkable, we must regard them as meaningless. Thus, what makes type predicates different from other predicates is not, as Pap claims, that their ranges of significance are unlimited. It is, as Russell and Carnap claim, that they designate their own ranges of significance.

In taking this view, it may be that I am blurring some important distinctions. For example, consider the following pairs of sentences:

(33) A thought is a spatially extended thing.
(34) The theory of relativity is a spatially extended thing.

(35) The class of all integers is a number.
(36) Socrates is a number.

Although all of these sentences are type crossings and are meaningless in the sense that we cannot understand what it would be like for them to be true, nevertheless, the second member of each pair is more clearly a type crossing and more clearly meaningless than the first member. One reason for this is that the crossing of types involved in the first member is more subtle, so that a person might be more easily misled into thinking that the sentence is true. There are also other reasons, which we need not go into. The important point, I think, is that when I say of false type predications that they are meaningless, I am not saying anything of them that would entail that they can never be profitably discussed or debated. Thus, although the meaninglessness of sentences (33) and (35) may not be so clear to some people, nevertheless, they *are* type crossings, just as sentence (27) ("a person's thoughts are in his brain"), though sometimes debated, is definitely a type crossing.

To summarize this chapter, I would say that the main difficulty with Ryle's theory is that it is too *inclusive,* making type crossings out of sentences such as (14)–(16), which we do not want to say are type crossings, or at least not allowing us to draw any clear distinction between such sentences and type crossings. On the other hand, the main difficulty with Pap's theory is that it is too *restrictive,* for it eliminates from the class of type crossings sentences, such as (34) and (36), which we are definitely inclined to say *are* type crossings.

It seems that what we need, then, is a theory of type crossings which avoids these extremes, one which is not as inclusive or vague as Ryle's theory nor as restrictive as Pap's theory. It is to the task of formulating such a theory that I turn now.

6

A NEW APPROACH

The question arises at this point: why can't we simply return to our working definition, according to which a type crossing is a sentence which says of one type of thing something that has application only to a different type of thing? At least this definition is neither too inclusive nor too restrictive. What is wrong with it, then, as a theory of type crossings?

The trouble comes when we want our theory to function as a criterion which can be applied to sentences in a *precise* way to determine whether or not they are type crossings. Because of a certain lack of preciseness, our working definition cannot be used with facility to exclude from the class of type crossings certain sentences which we want to exclude, such as (14)–(16). Furthermore, there are other sentences which we want to include in that class but which do not clearly meet the conditions imposed by our working definition, for example, sentences such as "quadruplicity drinks procrastination", "he had a green thought", "all green numbers are valid", and so on.

The main respects in which our working definition needs to be clarified in order for it to constitute an adequate criterion for type crossings can be formulated in terms of the following questions:

    I: What is it for something to "have application to" a type of thing?

    II: What is it for a sentence to "say something" of a type of thing?

    III: What is it for two things to be of "different type"?

Once these three questions are answered, we will have a basis for reformulating our working definition in a precise way, so that it may be regarded as an adequate criterion for type crossings.

6.1. THE BASIC FORMULATION

When it is said that a property "has application to" a type of thing, what this means is that there is a certain type, or general class of things, which is associated or connected in a certain way with that property. For example, the general class of things associated with the property of being blue is the class of spatially extended things. The exact nature of this "association" will be taken up later in the chapter. For the time being, let us put forward a rough reformulation of our working definition, as follows:

A type crossing is a sentence which ascribes to something of a certain type a property with which only a different type of thing is associated.[1]

This may be considered the "basic formulation" of our new theory of type crossings. I shall take it as a definition of what will be called "simple type crossings". Let us turn now to some considerations that need to be discussed in connection with the basic formulation.

Question II was: what is it for a sentence to "say something" of a type of thing? Phrasing it in terms of our basic formulation, we can put the question this way: what is it for a sentence to ascribe a property to something? In the case of subject-predicate type crossings, like "the theory of relativity is blue", there is no difficulty; we can see very easily how the basic formulation applies to them. But what about type crossings which are not of this simple subject-predicate form? That is the problem which must confront us now.

Consider, first of all, relational type crossings such as the following, taken from our original list:

(2) The number 5 weighs more than the number 6.
(4) Quadruplicity drinks procrastination.
(6) I have eaten a loud clap.
(8) Chemistry is a greater ordinal than the concept of truth.

[1] The word 'only' is to be understood here in such a way that the sentence entails that there definitely *is* a type of thing which is associated with the property in question.

In each of these cases, what is the property and what is the something to which it is ascribed? One possible approach is to break each sentence up into at least two sentences, replacing individual terms by the type-neutral word 'something'. Thus, (2) could be broken up into the following two sentences:

(2a) The number 5 weighs more than something.
(2b) Something weighs more than the number 6.

These may be considered entailments of the original sentence. We can say that (2a) ascribes to the number 5 the property of weighing more than something, a property with which only a different type of thing is associated. And (2b) entails a proposition which ascribes to the number 6 the property of weighing less than something, a property, again, with which only a different type of thing is associated.

There are several difficulties confronting this approach. One of them is that it becomes either impossible or else too difficult to handle when more complicated relational type crossings are considered, such as the following:

(37) Chemistry is swimming between the North Pole and the concept of truth.
(38) Numbers 1 through 7 are playing poker with one another.
(39) All numbers admire one another.

Although it might be possible to break up sentences (37) and (38) into parts in the manner illustrated with sentence (2), this would certainly be a difficult undertaking, especially with sentence (38). Furthermore, in the case of (39), it does not seem to be even possible to handle the sentence by this approach. There are also other objections, which we need not go into. It is clear, then, that this approach must be abandoned.

An alternative approach, which will be adopted in the present book, is that according to which relations are themselves regarded as properties which are ascribed to sets of things. Thus, in sentence (2), we say that the "two-place" property of "weighing more than" is ascribed to the ordered set: the number 5, the number 6. In sentence (37), the "three-place" property of "——— swimming between ——— and ———" is ascribed to the ordered set: chemistry, the North Pole, the concept of truth. Here, sets of things are themselves regarded as *things* which belong to one type or another. But then we seem to run into sets which have no properties at all, apart from the property of being a set, as in the case of the ordered set: chemistry, the North Pole, the concept of truth. I shall put off discussing this matter until Section 6.3, where, as we shall see, it presents certain obstacles to the definition of a "type of thing".

Sentences (38) and (39) have their own peculiarities. First, it should be noted that, unlike the previous examples, they do not involve *ordered* sets. Second, whereas the property involved in (39) is a "two-place" property (viz., "——— admires ———"), that involved in (38) (viz., "playing poker with one another") is a multi-placed property, ascribable to a set of indefinite size.[2] Neither of these points leads to any difficulties, so far as I can see.

Finally, (39) involves the universal quantifier 'all', which makes it impossible to enumerate the various sets of things to which the property "——— admires ———" is being ascribed. However, there is no reason why they should have to be enumerated. Since (39) ascribes to something of a certain type[3] (viz., all possible pairs of numbers) a property (the relation of admiring)

[2] It is not clear whether the statement that the members of a certain set are playing poker with one another entails that they are all playing in the same game (using just one deck of cards, of course) or whether it is compatible with the simultaneous occurrence of more than one game. But in either case there is a vague upper limit to the number of members who can be said to be "playing poker with one another". Nevertheless, the property in question is still indefinite with respect to the number of members within that limit to which the property is ascribable.

[3] By 'something of a certain type' is meant 'some member *or set of members* of a certain type'. In the case where the property is a relation, the "something" to which it is ascribed could be a set of sets, as for instance in those cases where the "something" is not enumerable. Thus, in sentence (39), the something to which the property is ascribed is the set of all pairs of numbers.

with which only a different type of thing is associated, it follows that (39) is a simple type crossing by virtue of our basic formulation. This same result would apply to all such sentences as "some numbers are green", "several numbers admire one another", etc. The fact that the "something" to which the property is ascribed cannot be enumerated does not present any difficulty. All that is required is that there be a certain *type* of which the "something" is either a member or a set of members. This notion of "type" will be discussed at length in Section 6.3. For the time being, I hope to have shown that relational type crossings, such as those considered above, can all be interpreted in such a way as to conform to our basic formulation. They are therefore to be regarded as simple type crossings. Also, in the remainder of the book, I shall continue to use the term "property' in the general sense which includes relations.

Let us now consider sentences containing negative predicates, such as the following:

(40) Socrates is not a person.
(41) Socrates is a non-person.
(42) Socrates is something other than a person.

The problem here is to interpret our basic formulation in such a way that these sentences are *excluded* from the class of simple type crossings. In order to do this, we have to understand that the ascription of properties to things which is referred to in the basic formulation must be done *in a positive manner*. Thus, any sentence which is of the form "S is not P",[4] or which is equivalent to a sentence of that form, is to be excluded from the class of simple type crossings, because its predicate is applied to its subject in a negative manner rather than in a positive manner.[5] In-

---

[4] Expressed in symbolic notation, the form is any in the following series: $\sim Fa$, $\sim R(a,b)$, $\sim R(a,b,c)$, ... Note that when the negation signs are dropped, this series expresses the forms to which our basic formulation is applicable, hence, the possible forms for simple type crossings.

[5] In the process of analyzing the form of a sentence to determine whether it denies a property to a thing or ascribes it in a positive manner, double negatives are to be assumed to cancel each other out. Thus, the sentence

stead of *ascribing* a property to a thing, such a sentence *denies* a property to a thing, which is something quite different. In order to bring out both this result and previous results in an explicit way, let us reformulate our basic formulation as follows:

A simple type crossing is a sentence which ascribes in a positive manner to a thing or set of things of a certain type a property with which only a different type of thing or set of things is associated.

Sentences (40)–(42) are excluded from the class of simple type crossings because they do not ascribe any property in a positive manner. (40) is of the form "S is not P", and (41) and (42) are equivalent to (40). Hence, all three ascribe their respective properties in a negative manner rather than in a positive manner, and so, fail to meet our basic formulation. On the other hand, there may be sentences which have the initial appearance of being negative, but which are not actually equivalent to any sentence of the form "S is not P". For example, "x is intolerant of carelessness" certainly says more than merely "x is not tolerant of carelessness". On this basis, both "the number 4 is tolerant of carelessness" and "the number 4 is intolerant of carelessness" are capable of being shown to be simple type crossings. In general, predicates beginning with 'in', 'im', 'un', etc., unlike the logicians' predicates beginning with 'non-', have a positive content, so that sentences containing them are not equivalent to any sentence of the form "S is not P". They *can* therefore be used to form simple type crossings.

6.2. COMPLEX TYPE CROSSINGS

Let us turn our attention now to still more complicated sentences, such as the following:

(43) Virtue is green and honesty is blue.
(44) Virtue is green or honesty is blue.
(45) If virtue is green, then the sky is both blue and not blue.

"Socrates is not something other than a prime number", when properly analyzed, turns out to be a simple type crossing. When the double negative is eliminated, it is seen to be equivalent to our familiar type crossing "Socrates is a prime number".

Considering sentence (43), we can see that our basic formulation can be easily applied to each clause, but not to the sentence as a whole. This might suggest an approach whereby (43) is classified as a type crossing on the grounds that it *entails* at least one simple type crossing. But such an approach will not do in the case of disjunctions, such as sentence (44), since they do not entail their individual clauses. Yet there is no more reason to regard (43) a type crossing than to regard (44) a type crossing. For this reason, it is preferable to apply the term 'type crossing' only to individual clauses or to subject-predicate sentences, and not to compound sentences made up of these. Thus, (43) and (44) are not to be called "type crossings". Rather, they should be referred to as "a conjunction of type crossings" and "a disjunction of type crossings", respectively. Sentence (45), in turn, should be referred to as "the implication of a non-type-crossing by a simple type crossing". That (45) should also be logically equivalent to the negation of the simple type crossing which it contains is an interesting feature of it, but not relevant to its correct classification.

Sometimes a sentence can be handled in more than one way. For example, the sentence "virtue is a green pitchfork" could be analyzed as a conjunction of type crossings: "virtue is green and virtue is a pitchfork". Or alternatively, it could be taken as a simple type crossing, ascribing to virtue the property of being a green pitchfork. In either case, it can be handled in terms of our previous discussion.

But now consider the following:

(46) That thing is both a prime number and green.

This sentence is quite different. It cannot be regarded as a conjunction of type crossings, for neither of its individual clauses would in that case be a type crossing. Nor can it be regarded as a simple type crossing, for the property it would be taken to ascribe (viz., being both a prime number and green) is not a property with which any type of thing is associated. Hence, (46) does not conform to the basic formulation. The sentence would

have been a simple type crossing if it had been expressed as follows:

(47) That thing which is a prime number is green.

But as it is, (46) does not seem to be a type crossing at all, for it
does not conform to our working definition of a type crossing.
It does not say of one type of thing something that has application only to a different type of thing. Rather, it ascribes to something two properties which do not have application to any one
type of thing.

On the other hand, there is a certain inclination to regard (46)
as involving a crossing of types, especially when one dwells upon
the close resemblance between (46) and (47). Yielding to this
inclination, we could specify a procedure to be followed in cases
in which two or more properties, designated by the predicate of
a sentence, are ascribed to something designated by the subject.
We could say that, in the case of such sentences, if importing all
of the properties except one into the subject could transform
the sentence into a simple type crossing, then the sentence itself
should be regarded as a "complex type crossing". Thus, since
(46) can be transformed into (47), which is a simple type crossing, by importing the property of being a prime number into the
subject, (46) is to be called a "complex type crossing". This also applies in the following examples:

(48) That thing is a prime number and is green and is a pitch-
     fork.
(49) That thing which is green and which is a pitchfork is a
     prime number.

Since (48), which is not a simple type crossing, can be transformed by means of the specified procedure into (49), which *is*
a simple type crossing, it follows that (48) is a complex type
crossing. In general, if a sentence which is not a simple type
crossing can be transformed into one which either is a simple
type crossing or contains a simple type crossing as a clause by
means of some simple grammatical reformulation which does in

no way affect the content of the sentence, then the sentence is to be regarded as a "complex type crossing".

Let us try this out on a couple of examples suggested by Ziff and Strawson, namely:

(50) He had a green thought.
(51) There is a loud smell in the drawing-room.

Here, it is not the sentence itself which, so to speak, crosses types, but only an individual expression within the sentence. So there is no simple type crossing involved at all. The sentence iself is not a simple type crossing because it does not conform to our basic formulation. Nor is the individual expression (i.e., 'green thought' or 'loud smell') a simple type crossing, for it is not itself a sentence. However, we can reformulate the sentences in the following way:

(52) A certain thought is green and he had it.
(53) A certain smell is loud and it is in the drawing-room.

Admittedly, sentences (52) and (53) are rather awkward. But they do not differ in *content* from sentences (50) and (51), respectively. So, since (52) and (53) each contain a simple type crossing as a clause (namely, the first clause in each), it follows that (50) and (51) both conform to our general definition of a "complex type crossing".

However, not every sentence which we are inclined to say "involves" a type crossing can be handled in this way. For example, consider the following sentence:

(54) All green numbers are valid.

We would like to be able to say that (54) is a complex type crossing, but, in fact, it does not conform to our definition. We might try to revise the definition so as to include (54), but there is little point in such a procedure. No matter how we try to define 'complex type crossing' along these lines, it seems that there will always be exceptions. The possible structures for English sentences are just too numerous to be covered in any one formula. For this reason, it seems best to abandon the attempt to define the notion of a complex type crossing in terms of "grammatical reformulations".

Perhaps we could understand the notion of a complex type crossing in a loose way as a sentence which is not itself a simple type crossing, but which "contains" at least one simple type crossing. Thus, sentences (46), (50), (51), and (54) all "contain", in some vague way, at least one simple type crossing, and on this basis could be called "complex type crossings".

An obvious objection to this "loose" approach is that sentences (43)–(45) turn out to be complex type crossings, for they *contain* simple type crossings as explicit clauses. Yet those sentences were not supposed to be called "type crossings". Now, in the case of (43) and (44), I have no objection to calling the sentences "complex type crossings". But I agree that the label is not properly applied to (45). This, then, is the difficulty confronting the definition of 'complex type crossing' in terms of "containment": sentence (45) is certainly not a complex type crossing nor any sort of type crossing, yet it *contains* a simple type crossing as an explicit clause. What are we to say?

One might think that we could simply take sentences which are logically equivalent to the negations of simple type crossings, such as (45), as exceptions. In other words, that we could define complex type crossings as "sentences which contain simple type crossings except for those which are logically equivalent to the negations of simple type crossings". But this will not do, for we want to also exclude the negations of complex type crossings, such as the negations of sentences (46), (50), (51), and (54). We do not want to call them "type crossings" at all, yet, without further clarification, it seems we must take them to "contain" simple type crossings just as their positive counterparts do. Nor can we insert into the definition of 'complex type crossing' any clause which excludes them (or sentences logically equivalent to them), for that would make the definition circular. That is, 'complex type crossing' would then be defined in part in terms of the expression 'negation of complex type crossing'. How are we to escape this difficulty?

One possibility might be to abandon the notion of "containment" and go back to our very first suggestion, the appeal to the concept of entailment. Thus, suppose we were to define a complex type crossing as a sentence which is not itself a simple type crossing, but which *entails* at least one simple type crossing. This definition would have the advantage of eliminating in one stroke both the difficulty about the negations of type crossings and the reference to the vague notion of "containment". But this definition is, after all, no more than a special form of the "grammatical reformulation" criterion. As might be expected, it suffers from its own peculiar difficulties. First of all, as has been pointed out previously, sentence (44) does not conform to the definition, whereas (43) does. To call (43) a type crossing, but not (44), runs counter to our intuitions about the matter. Secondly, sentence (54), which we found does not meet the "grammatical reformulation" criterion, does not meet this one either. That is, (54) does not entail any simple type crossing. Yet, if we are going to specify a class of complex type crossings at all, I should think (54) is one of the sentences we would want to include in that class. And finally, there is the standard difficulty about all appeals to the concept of entailment, namely, that self-contradictory sentences entail *anything*. Therefore, by this definition, any self-contradictory sentence would turn out to be a complex type crossing. I think these difficulties are sufficiently formidable to warrant our abandonment, once and for all, of this "entailment approach".

Let us consider another possibility, one which makes appeal to the technical apparatus of symbolic logic. Suppose our complex type crossings were to be translated into the notation of quantifiers, variables, and truth-functional constants. Then we could say that a clause or subject-predicate sentence is a complex type crossing if its translation involves the application of incompatible predicates to a given variable in a negation-free context (i.e., without the appearance of negation signs before any of the incompatible predicates). For example, consider sentence (54). Translating this into the language of symbolic logic, we get the following: "for any x, if x is green and x is a number, then x is valid". Since all these predicates, 'being green', 'being a number', and 'being valid', are mutually incompatible, and since they are all applied to a single variable (namely, 'x') in a negation-free context, it follows that (54) is a complex type crossing. Consider another example. Translating sentence (50) into the symbolic language, we get the following: "there exists at least one x such that x is green and x is a thought and x is had by him". Here it is just 'is green' and 'is a thought' which are incompatible predicates, but since they are both applied to the same variable in a negation-free context, it follows that (50) conforms to the definition of a complex type crossing.

It should be noted that this approach can also be applied to sentences which we have taken as simple type crossings. Consider, for example, sentence (39) ("all numbers admire one another"). This would be analyzed as: "for any pair, x and y, if x and y are numbers, then x admires y". Here, the predicates 'are numbers' and 'admires' are applied to the same pair of variables, x and y, in a negation-free context. And since they are incompatible predicates, it follows that (39) is a complex type crossing. That a sentence should be both a complex type crossing and a simple type crossing does not, so far as I can see, lead to any difficulties.

It might be objected, however, that the approach we are considering would admit as a complex type crossing a sentence which we do not want to admit, namely, sentence (14) ("some red things are all green"). This sentence would be translated as: "there exists at least one x such that x is red and x is all green." Here, so the objection goes, the incompatible predicates 'is red' and 'is all green' are applied to the same variable, 'x', and so the sentence conforms to the criterion for a complex type crossing. However, the predicates 'is red' and 'is all green' are not incompatible in the same way in which the predicates used in the previous examples are incompatible. For one thing, although

it is impossible for a thing to be both red and all green at the
same time, it is not impossible for it to have those properties at
different times. For example, leaves are all green in the summer,
but red in the fall. On the other hand, it *is* impossible for anything to, say, be green and be a thought, even at different times.
So, it is a feature of properties which are incompatible in the
sense in which we are interested that no one thing can have
them, even at different times. Nevertheless, this is not the crucial
distinction that we seek, for it does not enable us to exclude
from the class of complex type crossings certain other sentences
which we want to exclude, such as "some totally reflexive relations are intransitive" and "some even numbers greater than 2
are prime numbers". The distinction between such sentences and
complex type crossings, like "some thoughts are green", is this:
whereas the type associated with being green does not contain any
thoughts as members, the type associated with, say, being a prime
number *does* contain even numbers greater than 2 as members, that type being the class of natural numbers. Let us bring
out this difference by calling the sort of incompatibility that
exists between 'is green' and 'is a thought' (or between the properties of being green and being a thought) "type incompatibility". Thus, although the predicates 'is red' and 'is all green', and
'is an even number greater than 2' and 'is a prime number', are
in some sense incompatible, they are not "type incompatible".
We can now express our definition of a complex type crossing in
terms of the concept of type incompatibility:

A complex type crossing is a sentence whose translation into the
language of symbolic logic applies predicates to a variable in a negation-free context which are type incompatible. And two predicates
are type incompatible if and only if they designate properties at least
one of which has associated with it a type none of whose members
has the other property.[6]

---

[6] It must be understood here that the reason they do not have the other
property is *not* that nothing has it (as in the case of "some prime numbers
divisible by 2 are even numbers", which is not a type crossing). Nor are
we to say that the reason is invariably that they do not belong to the type

What I have given is just an outline or suggestion. Certainly much more needs to be done in order for this approach to complex type crossings to be developed in full. And it may very well turn out that, like the other attempts to define 'complex type crossing' in a precise way, it too will succumb to insuperable difficulties. If that should happen, it seems our only alternative would be to return to the vague notion of "containment". We would have to say something to the effect that complex type crossings are sentences which are not themselves simple type crossings but which "contain" simple type crossings *in a positive way*. We would then have to understand this notion of "containment in a positive way" in such a way that sentences logically equivalent to the negations of either simple or complex type crossings are *not* taken to contain simple type crossings in a positive way. As was indicated earlier, if we insert this proviso into the explicit definition of a complex type crossing, the definition would turn out circular. Perhaps some way might be found to formulate the definition in a recursive manner so that the circularity could be avoided, but I do not see offhand how that could be done. It seems, then, that the notion of "containment in a positive way" must be understood in some intuitive manner which permits complex type crossings to contain simple type crossings in a positive way, but which does not permit their negations to do so. To define 'complex type crossing' in terms of such an obscure notion of course makes the concept of a complex type crossing itself obscure, but perhaps that is as it should be. If the "incompatible predicates" approach should fail, then there is no reason at all to believe that the concept should have to be precise.

Before concluding this section, something should be said about sentences which do not so much "contain" simple type crossings as *presuppose* them. I have in mind such examples as the following:

(55) The brightness of triangularity is distressing.

---

associated with the other property, for that would exclude "some imaginary numbers are prime numbers", which *is* a type crossing.

(56) Honesty is admired by every other logician.[7]

These sentences presuppose the following simple type crossings, respectively:

(57) Triangularity is bright.
(58) Honesty is a logician.

Let us think of sentences such as (55) and (56) as being in a special category which we could refer to by the name "presuppositional type crossings". Such type crossings are in a class by themselves for two reasons. First, they do not conform to any of the definitions of 'complex type crossing' which have been considered. And second, they have a feature which is peculiar to them, namely, the fact that their negations are also (presuppositional) type crossings. For example, the negations of (55) and (56) presuppose the simple type crossings (57) and (58), just as do (55) and (56) themselves. It follows that they should also be regarded as presuppositional type crossings. I see no difficulties in this. Let us say, then, that there are *three* categories of type crossings: simple, complex, and presuppositional.

A certain objection now needs to be disposed of. It may be claimed that the negations of certain simple type crossings can now be introduced as (presuppositional) type crossings because they "presuppose" false type predications (which we decided in Chapter 5 to regard as type crossings). For example, "the theory of relativity is not blue" presupposes, according to this argument, "the theory of relativity is a spatially extended thing", which is a simple type crossing. Hence, "the theory of relativity is not blue", which is a sentence we do not want to classify as a type crossing of any sort, turns out to be a presuppositional type crossing. My reply to this is to point out that the relation between (55) and (57), or between (56) and (58), is a quite different sort of relation, for in these cases there is a specific word which is explicitly used to signify the presupposition. In sentence (55),

---

[7]   This sentence is to be understood apart from any special context, so that the term 'other' means 'other than that which is designated by the subject (which in this case is 'honesty')'.

it is the purpose of the word 'the' to signify an acceptance of (57). And in sentence (56), it is the purpose of the word 'other' to signify an acceptance of (58). In contrast, "the theory of relativity is not blue" does not contain any word whose purpose in the sentence is to signify an acceptance of "the theory of relativity is a spatially extended thing". Therefore, it does not presuppose the latter sentence in the sense relevant to "presuppositional type crossings". The expression "X presupposes Y" is to be taken to mean "X contains a specific term whose purpose in X is to signify an acceptance of Y". As long as the notion of "presupposing", which is used to define 'presuppositional type crossing', is understood in this sense, the introduction of presuppositional type crossings as a special class of type crossings will be immune to the sort of objection considered above.

Section 6.2 has been a diversion from our main task in the present chapter, which is to try to make our working definition of a type crossing more precise. The discussion of complex and presuppositional type crossings is irrelevant to that task, for such sentences do not conform to the working definition of a type crossing. Rather, the only sentences which conform to that definition are those which also conform to our basic formulation of Section 6.1. Thus, it is only simple type crossings which are type crossings in the sense used so far throughout this book. Although complex type crossings "contain" type crossings in a way that is either clear or obscure, depending on the ultimate success of the "incompatible predicates" approach, they are not themselves type crossings in the sense specified by our working definition. And this applies also to presuppositional type crossings. We must now return to our main task, for it will be seen that the basic formulation stands in need of further clarification.

6.3. TYPES AND TYPE DIFFERENCES

Certain questions need to be raised about the nature of types and type differences. What is a type? And, as in Question III, what is it for two things to be of different type? We say that "the theory of relativity is blue" is a type crossing because the theory of relativity belongs to a type which is not associated with the property of being blue, whereas there is a different type which *is* associated with that property and to which the theory of relativity does *not* belong. The first type is perhaps the class of sets of propositions, and the second type is the class of spatially extended things. But how do we *know* what types the theory of relativity belongs to or does not belong to? And what makes two types different?

Following the outline presented by Arthur Pap, let us initially define a "type" as the range of significance of a given predicate, that is, the class of things (or class of sets of things) to which the property designated by the predicate can meaningfully be ascribed. For example, the type associated with the predicate 'is blue' is the class of spatially extended things; the type associated with 'is a prime number' is the class of natural numbers; the type associated with the relational predicate 'weighs more than' is the class of pairs of physical objects; the type associated with 'drinks' is the class of ordered pairs the first member of which is an organism with a mouth and the second member of which is a liquid. We can then go on to say that two types are different if they have different members, and they are the same if they have the same members.

But now a certain difficulty arises. According to our basic formulation:

a simple type crossing is a sentence which ascribes in a positive manner to a thing or set of things *of a certain type* a property with which only a different type of thing or set of things is associated.

However, if 'type' is to mean 'range of significance of a predicate', then in the case of sets of things, there may not be any type to which the set belongs. For example, consider the ordered set "quadruplicity, procrastination", which is the "subject" of sentence (4). In this case there may not exist a class and a predicate such that the set "quadruplicity, procrastination" is a member of the class, and the predicate is meaningfully applicable to all and only members of that class. This may also be the case with the ordered set "chemistry, the North Pole, the concept of truth", which is the "subject" of sentence (37), and with an indefinite number of other sets.

It may be suggested that there *is* a type to which all these sets belong, namely, the class of all sets. The class of all sets is a type because 'is a set' is a type predicate and thereby designates its own range of significance. In other words, all and only sets can meaningfully be said to *be sets*. Thus, the class of sets is the range of significance of the predicate 'is a set' and, therefore, is a type. However, this will not work, because the type associated with the relational property of drinking, to which the set "quadruplicity, procrastination" does not belong, is not a *different type* from the class of all sets, but rather, is a subclass of it. The class of all sets, then, is simply not relevant to this case, for, although it is a type, and although the set "quadruplicity, procrastination" does belong to it, we still could not say that the set in question belongs to a type which is *different* from that associated with the property of drinking. Thus, some other way out of the difficulty must be sought.

It may be pointed out that it is not necessary that the thing or set of things which is not of the right type to have a certain property should itself be of some type or other. It may be that, in fact, every thing and every set of things *is* a member of some type or other, but this fact is in no way necessary for our purposes. For this reason, it is sufficient that we express our basic formulation a little more loosely, as follows:

A simple type crossing is a sentence which ascribes in a positive manner to a thing or set of things, x, a property with which the type of thing or set of things associated is a class to which x does not belong.

Thus, in order for "quadruplicity drinks procrastination" to be a type crossing, all that is necessary is that the set "quadruplicity, procrastination" not be a member of the type of set of things associated with the property of drinking. And for this, the sentence easily qualifies. However, this approach raises still another difficulty, which may be brought out by reference to one of the sentences mentioned back on page 34. The sentence is the following:

(13) An entity which is not a number is a number.

The reason given for denying that (13) is a type crossing was that "there is nothing about the class of things which are not of a given type that warrants saying that it is itself a type of thing". But now if we no longer require that what a type crossing is about be itself a member of some type or other, then it seems (13) might qualify as a type crossing; and we certainly do not want that. Clearly, then, some restriction must be placed on the "thing or set ot things" to which the property in a type crossing is ascribed, but it must not be any restriction which would eliminate those sets which do not belong to any relevant type. I think the restriction we need is that the "thing or set of things" be something *specific*, i.e., something that is not a general class which cuts across type boundaries and includes things of many different types. This restriction eliminates sentence (13), for the expression 'entity which is not a number' clearly does not designate anything that is specific in the required sense.[8] On the other hand, the restriction does not eliminate sentences such as (4) and (37), for their logical subjects *are* quite specific. Nor does it eliminate a sentence such as (39) ("all numbers admire one another"), for, although the subject in this case is a general class, it is not a general class which contains things of many different types; hence, it is specific in that sense of 'specific' introduced above. This approach apparently avoids the difficulty in question without introducing any difficulties of its own.

---

[8] This same restriction can be applied to our troublesome sentence (11) ("an abstract entity is a concrete entity") in order to eliminate it from the class of type crossings, for the expression 'abstract entity' does cut across type boundaries and does cover things of many different types. Therefore, that expression does not designate anything specific in the required sense of 'specific'. It follows, then, that sentence (11) is not a type crossing. Thus, our generalization that no type crossings are self-contradictory can be maintained as unexceptionable after all.

The only change that needs to be made in our basic formulation is the insertion of the word 'specific' before each occurrence of the word 'thing'. Since there are no difficulties involved in doing this, we may regard our problem solved. However, we are still confronted by the problem of understanding the concept of a type.

We said that a type is the class of things (or class of sets of things) to which a given property can be meaningfully ascribed. But what is the test for whether or not a property can be meaningfully ascribed to a thing? There does not seem to be any useful non-circular criterion to which we can appeal here. Let us therefore turn to an approach which bypasses the appeal to meaningfulness altogether.

The approach I have in mind is that according to which the type associated with a given property is the class of things (or class of sets of things) which can *thinkably* have that property.[9] For example, the type associated with the property of being blue is the class of things which can thinkably be blue (which turns out to be the class of spatially extended things). And since it is unthinkable for the theory of relativity to be blue, the theory of relativity must fall outside the type associated with the property of being blue. Hence, "the theory of relativity is blue" is a type crossing. The test for whether or not a given thing can thinkably have a certain property is to try to think of it as having that property, that is, to try to put the concept of that thing and the concept of that property together in thought. If you fail, then the proposition that the thing has the property is an unthinkable proposition (i.e., an unthinkable combination of concepts). If you succeed, then the proposition *is* thinkable, and the sentence ascribing the property to the thing is *not* a type crossing.

Consider the application of this approach to sentence (14)

[9]   This reference to thinkability is in itself not historically new. Arthur Pap probably had some such concept in mind when he spoke about "intuition". (See the quotation on pages 84-85, above.) Then there is also Ryle's assertion: "what is absurd is unthinkable" ("Categories", p. 201; Flew, p. 76). But the use of such a concept in the context of an explicit theory of type crossings *is* something new.

("Some red things are all green"). What is the type associated with being all green? Is it the class of things which are all green or is it the class of spatially extended things? In the former case, (14) would be a type crossing. In the latter case, it would not be a type crossing. To decide the matter, we need to ask whether it is thinkable for a spatially extended thing which is not all green to be all green. The answer is "Yes". We can even cite examples. Leaves in the fall are not all green, yet it is certainly thinkable that they should be. We need only imagine them to be the way they were in the summer in order to think of them as being all green. So we can conclude, then, that the type associated with being all green, according to the "thinkability approach", is the class of spatially extended things. Hence, sentence (14), by this approach, is not a type crossing. This conforms nicely with our intuitions about types.

There is, however, one great difficulty with the thinkability approach which must now be taken up. The difficulty can be brought out in terms of the following sentence:

(59) The number 4 is greater than the number 5.

According to the thinkability approach, the type associated with the relation 'is greater than' (taken in the arithmetical sense) is the class of pairs of numbers, the first of which is greater than the second (that is, the relation is itself a type property). The reason for this is that it is unthinkable for a number which is not greater than a given number to be greater than it. If someone were to claim that he could think of the number 4 as being greater than the number 5, we would have to regard him as having made a mistake of some sort (probably a vocabulary mistake). Thus, the proposition expressed by sentence (59) is an unthinkable proposition. And since the ordered pair "the number 4, the number 5" does not, therefore, belong to the type which, according to the thinkability approach, is associated with the relation of being greater than, it follows that sentence (59) is a type crossing. However, this result does not at all square with our intuitions about types. We want to say that the type associated with the relation of being greater than is simply the class of pairs of real numbers. And since the pair "the number 4, the number 5" is a member of that class, it follows that sentence (59) is *not* a type crossing.

The advocate of the thinkability approach has, as I see it, two possible responses to this objection. In order to discuss these, let us first introduce a distinction between two sorts of properties: essential properties and accidental properties. A property is essential if every sentence ascribing it to a thing or set of things is an a priori sentence. It is accidental if at least one of the sentences is empirical. However, it must be understood that the subject of the sentence in each case is something other than a descriptive phrase (or a phrase which leaves doubt as to what the subject represents). This would eliminate from consideration such sentences as "the number of marbles in this box is a prime number", which is empirical, even though the property it ascribes (i.e., being a prime number) is an essential property. In general, essential properties are those encountered in logic and mathematics, although most type properties are also essential. They are properties without which the things that have them could not be what they are. On the other hand, a thing need not have its accidental properties, as, for example, color properties and measurable properties. A thing would still be what it is even if it were not red or green or three feet long or weighing five pounds, etc. Such properties could change and the thing would still be the same thing. But in the case of essential properties, such as being a prime number, being a valid argument, being a symmetrical relation, being a spatially extended thing, etc., a thing which has the property cannot give it up and still be the same thing. For example, a number cannot change from odd to even, or vice versa, and still *be* the same number. Thus, being odd and being even are essential properties.

We can now draw a distinction between accidental and essential type crossings which corresponds to that between accidental and essential properties. An accidental type crossing is a simple type crossing which ascribes an accidental property to something. An essential type crossing is a simple type crossing which ascribes an essential property to something. It can be seen that developing a theory of essential type crossing may be quite a different undertaking from that of developing a theory of accidental type crossings.

The advocate of the thinkability approach has these two possible courses open to him: either he can dogmatically continue to apply the thinkability test to essential properties, in which case he will have to maintain the peculiar result that all essential properties are type properties, or else he can apply the thinkability test only to accidental properties, leaving essential properties to some other approach. As I see it, only the latter alternative is at all feasible, but there are still enormous problems confronting it, especially in the construction of an adequate theory of essential type crossings.

Consider, first of all, the former line of defense. Suppose the advocate of the thinkability approach were to argue in the following way. The type associated with a property is the range of significance of the property, i.e., the class of things to which the property can be meaningfully ascribed. But essential properties can be meaningfully ascribed only to things which have them. It makes no sense to say of the number 4, for example, that it is a prime number, or an odd number, or that it is greater than the number 5. We simply cannot understand what it would be like for any of these propositions to be true. They are all unthinkable. Therefore, the number 4 must fall outside of the range of significance of each of the properties in question. And, in fact, everything must fall outside of those ranges of significance except for the things which actually have the given property. In other words, only prime numbers can meaningfully be said to be prime numbers, only odd numbers can meaningfully be said to be odd numbers, and only pairs of numbers in which the first is greater than the second can meaningfully be said to have the relation of being greater than. Therefore, all essential properties are type properties. The type associated with them is none other than the class of things which have them.

This result is not at all satisfying. It entails the rather odd conclusion that sentences such as the following are type crossings:

(60) The square of 181 is greater than the cube of 32.
(61) 1739 is a prime number.

Yet, surely we are inclined to draw a distinction between these two sentences and the following two:

(62) The concept of truth is greater than my left eye.
(63) Procrastination is a prime number.

We want to say that although the square of 181 and the cube of 32 are not in fact related by the property of the first being greater than the second, nevertheless they are the *type* of set that could be so related, namely, a pair of real numbers. Similarly, although 1739 is not in fact a prime number (being the product of 37 and 47), nevertheless it is the *type* of thing associated with being a prime number, namely, a natural number. To deny this is to give up all point to the concept of a type, for what point could the concept have if not to draw such distinctions as between (60) and (62), and as between (61) and (63)?

It is true that there is a sense of 'meaningless' in which (60) and (61) are meaningless, namely, that sense which is defined in terms of unthinkability. However, that is clearly *not* the sense to which we appeal in our definition of 'type'. On the contrary, it seems that we must appeal to some other approach in order to define the type or "range of significance" of an essential property. Thus, we have seen how the defense of the thinkability approach which was suggested above can be easily broken down. Since the application of that approach to essential properties leads to counter-intuitive results, such an application must be abandoned.

We come now to what appears to be the last course open to us, namely, to define "type associated with an accidental property" in terms of the thinkability approach and to define "type associated with an essential property" in terms of some other approach. What, then, might that other approach be? As a first stab, let us introduce the notion of a subject matter (or realm of discourse). A class of things will be said to constitute a subject matter if and only if: (1) it presents its own special problems, (2) it is studied by investigators, (3) theories are developed about it, and (4) its members have important properties in common which are not possessed by other things. The type associated with an essential property can now be defined as the smallest class of things (or sets of things) which constitutes a subject matter and to which everything which has the property belongs.[10]

Thus, the type associated with the property of being a prime number is the class of natural numbers, for the class of natural numbers is the smallest class of things which constitutes a subject matter and which contains all prime numbers. Although the class of odd numbers plus the number 2 is a still smaller class containing all prime numbers, it does not meet the four conditions for constituting a subject matter, and hence does not qualify as a *type*. But what about the class of prime numbers itself? Why is that not the type associated with being a prime number (in which case being a prime number would be a type property)? The reason is, again, that the class does not meet all the conditions for constituting a subject matter. The class of prime numbers may be on the borderline of meeting the first three conditions (or it may be said to meet those conditions on a small scale), but it does not meet the fourth condition, which requires of a subject matter that its members share important properties not possessed by other things. One of the main reasons for this is that the class of prime numbers is not divided into nonarbitrary subclasses (i.e., subclasses which are not merely arbitrary inventions such as "the class of prime numbers between 100 and 200", etc.). The disjunctive property of being either in one nonarbitrary

[10] It may be suggested that a further condition needs to be specified, namely, that the class be usually thought of in connection with the given property, or be "mentally associated" with it. It may very well be that some such condition as this needs to be added, but, at the moment, it strikes me as being superfluous. I cannot think of any class which meets the original conditions but does not meet this one as well.

subclass or another may be regarded as an *important* property of members of a given class. For example, the property of being either odd or even is an important property of natural numbers. The property of being either rational or irrational is an important property of real numbers. The property of being either symmetrical or asymmetrical or nonsymmetrical is an important property of relations. We can say, then, that one of the main reasons why prime numbers do not share any important properties not possessed by other things is that they do not have any such disjunctive properties. Of course, all prime numbers share the property of being a prime number itself, together with whatever other properties are entailed by it (such as "not being divisible by 3", etc.). But these are not justifiably regarded as important properties. If they really were important properties, then there would no doubt be more inclination than exists now to regard the class of prime numbers itself as the type associated with being a prime number, and thus to regard false sentences such as "1739 is a prime number" as type crossings.

As a further illustration of how the subject matter approach is to be applied, consider sentence (15), in which the property of being a symmetrical relation is ascribed to temporal precedence. There can be little doubt that the type associated with that property (i.e., the smallest class which constitutes a subject matter and to which all symmetrical relations belong) is the class of relations. But temporal precedence is a member of that class. It follows, then, that sentence (15) is not a type crossing. And this result is in accord with our intuitions about the matter.

It might be suggested that in the case of mathematical properties it could be a matter of calculation whether or not a given sentence is a type crossing. For example, consider the following sentences:

(64) The cube root of 4913 is a prime number.
(65) The cube root of 13813 is a prime number.
(66) The cube root of 19683 is a prime number.

Calculation yields the result that (64) is true, (65) is a type crossing (since its subject is not a natural number), and (66), though false, is not a type crossing (since its subject *is* a natural number). Even if the type associated with being a prime number were taken as the class of *real* numbers, rather than the class of natural numbers, calculation could still be involved, as in the following examples:

(67) $\sqrt{(181)^2 - (32)^3}$ is a prime number.

(68) $\sqrt{(32)^3 - (181)^2}$ is a prime number.

It is immediately evident that one subject must designate a real number and the other an imaginary number (barring the possibility that they both designate zero). Hence, one sentence would be a type crossing and the other not. Calculation must be appealed to in order to determine which is which. Although this result may sound a bit odd at first, I do not see how it could lead to any serious difficulties for our theory of type crossings. Thus, the suggestion strikes me as acceptable. All it comes to is the innocuous fact that calculation is sometimes required in order to see what is really being asserted by means of a given sentence.

A certain qualification must be made in the case of types of sets of things. We would no doubt like to say that the type associated with the relation of being greater than (in the arithmetical sense) is the class of pairs of real numbers. But in what sense can a class of *pairs* constitute a subject matter? It seems that we need to stretch the notion of a type to include not only classes which constitute subject matters, but also classes of *sets* made up from members of the classes which constitute subject matters. Thus, since the class of real numbers constitutes a subject matter, the class of pairs of real numbers meets our qualification, and hence can itself be regarded as a type. This same result can be extended to all other essential relations and the types of sets associated with them.

Unfortunately, there are many difficulties confronting the subject matter approach, especially in the area of mathematical properties. For example, according to the subject matter approach, the type associated with the property of being a prime number is the class of natural numbers. This in itself is to some extent counter-intuitive, for we are not inclined to draw such distinctions as between sentences (65) and (66), saying that one is a type crossing but not the other. But leaving this matter aside, there is now the further difficulty about determining the type associated with the property of being a natural number. If we follow the suggestion made at the end of Chapter 5, we would say that it is the class of natural numbers itself, for type predicates denote their own ranges of significance. This is also the result we get by application of the subject matter approach. Having classified the class of natural numbers as a subject matter, naturally it must be the smallest class which constitutes a subject matter and which contains all natural numbers. However, if we follow this approach, then we are led still further from what is intuitive. This can be seen in the case of the following sentences:

(69) The cube root of 13813 is a natural number.
(70) The cube root of 19683 is a natural number.

We would have to say that (69) is a type crossing but not (70). But this is surely going too far. We must not get into the position of saying that (69) is a type crossing. Although the sentence is false, it clearly does not involve a crossing of types. So what are we to say, then?

Two possibilities present themselves, but, as will be seen, neither of them is satisfactory. The first is to try to avoid the difficulty by drawing a distinction between meaning and reference. Let us illustrate this distinction, first of all, by applying it to another example. Suppose I write "3½" on a piece of paper and then announce the following:

(71) The number I have written down is a prime number.

Assuming that the sentence "3½ is a prime number" is a type crossing, is my utterance, (71), also a type crossing? The answer is that it is *not* a type crossing, because, although its subject, "the number I have written down", has the number 3½ as its *referent,* it does not have that number as its *meaning.* And it is the meaning to which we appeal in determining what "thing" a property is supposed to be ascribed to.[11] In the case of (71), the thing to which the property of being a prime number is ascribed is simply the concept which is *connoted* by "the number I have written down". This is a general concept which applies to all numbers expressible in writing. In this respect, (71) can be seen to be in many ways similar to the sentence "some numbers are prime numbers". Neither of them is a type crossing. To return, now, to our problematic sentence, (69), we can say that, although "the cube root of 13813" *refers* to some irrational number close to 23.99 . . ., nevertheless, that is not its *meaning*. Furthermore, its meaning is a general concept which includes natural numbers (though it is not clear exactly which ones), and therefore, (69) is not a type crossing. Now, there are at least two objections to this approach to the problem. First of all, the distinction between meaning and reference in the case of sentence (69) is not as clear as in the case of (71). Whereas it is an *empirical* matter whether or not "the number I have written down" refers to the number $3\frac{1}{2}$, it is *not* an empirical matter whether or not "the cube root of 13813" refers to a certain irrational number close to 23.99. . . Thus, the distinction between meaning and reference in the latter case is suspect. Secondly, even if the issue about meaning and reference were completely eliminated, the original problem would still remain. Let us suppose, for example, that our problematic sentence were the following:

(72) The number $3\frac{1}{2}$ is a natural number.

It is still counter-intuitive to regard (72) as a type crossing. Therefore, since the meaning-reference dichotomy is not relevant here, some other way out of the difficulty must be sought.

The second possibility would be to redefine the type associated with a given essential property as the smallest class constituting

---

[11] Sometimes the meaning of a term and its referent coalesce, as in the case of proper names. Thus, in "Socrates is a prime number", the thing to which the property is ascribed is the meaning of the subject term, which in this case also happens to be the referent of the term.

a subject matter to which everything which has the property belongs *and which is not equal to the class of things having that property.* When this proviso is added, we are obliged to regard the type associated with being a natural number to be some class other than the class of natural numbers. Presumably, it would turn out to be the class of real numbers. But, furthermore, the proviso obliges us to deny that *any* essential type predicate could denote its own type (or range of significance). This approach, then, runs up against the objection that there are at least some essential type predicates which *do* denote their own ranges of significance (e.g., 'is a relation', 'is a number', 'is a set', and so on). Furthermore, we do not get the best results with the property of being a natural number either. As was mentioned, the type associated with that property would presumably turn out to be the class of real numbers. But then we would have to say that a sentence such as "3i is a natural number" is a type crossing, which, I believe, is still counter-intuitive. It seems to me that the type associated with being a natural number should be the general class of numbers (including both real numbers and imaginary numbers). Yet, I see no way at all in which this result can be obtained by way of the subject matter approach. In conclusion, then, it seems that the subject matter approach is incapable of satisfactorily handling types associated with mathematical properties.

But there are still more basic objections to the subject matter approach than this. One that has great philosophical significance is the objection that the subject matter approach makes the concept of an essential type crossing *time-dependent.* That is, since whether or not a class is a subject matter is relative to human interests, it seems that what is a subject matter today may not have been a subject matter, say, 5000 years ago. Hence, what is a type crossing today probably would not have been a type crossing 5000 years ago. Consider, for example, the following sentence:

(73) Socrates is a symmetrical relation.

Since the type associated with being a symmetrical relation is the class of relations, and since Socrates falls outside that class, it follows that (73) is a type crossing. But since the class of relations was not a subject matter 5000 year ago, it seems that (73) probably would not have been a type crossing 5000 years ago. Thus, the subject matter approach makes the properties of being a type and being a type crossing *accidental* properties. It seems to entail, furthermore, that before there were any human beings to take an interest in certain classes of things, there were no types! Yet, this runs counter to our inclinations on the matter. We want to say that whether or not a sentence (understood in a certain way) is a type crossing is not time-dependent, but is an essential property of the sentence (understood in that way). And whether or not a class is a type relative to a given property is not time-dependent either, but is an essential property of the class. Since the subject matter approach makes both of these issues time-dependent and makes the corresponding properties accidental rather than essential, it is inadequate as a theory of type crossings.

The objection may also be applied to *future* possibilities. The subject matter approach seems to allow the possibility that the smallest class which will constitute a subject matter and which contains, say, all prime numbers will in the future be a class other than the class of natural numbers. For example, it may eventually become the class of prime numbers itself. Let us understand just what is involved in this supposition. In order for the class of prime numbers to become the type associated with being a prime number, it would have to become a subject matter. That is, it would have to present its own special problems, be studied by investigators, and have theories developed about it. As has been pointed out previously, all of these features already apply to the class of prime numbers on a small scale. What prevents the class of prime numbers from being a subject matter is its failure to meet the fourth condition, namely, that its members have *important* properties in common which are not possessed by other things. But suppose that in the future new discoveries in number theory should reveal important distinctions among different subclasses of prime numbers. Then such subclasses would be nonarbitrary, and, as a result, prime numbers would have the important property of being either in one nonarbitrary subclass or another (just as natural numbers have the important property of being either odd or even). Of course, we cannot imagine what such new discoveries might consist in, but we must concede that it is at least *possible* that they should take place. At any rate, such new developments would cause mathematicians to take a renewed interest in the theory of prime numbers, and, as a result, the class of prime numbers would come to meet all the conditions for being a subject matter. It would then follow, according to the subject matter approach, that the class of prime numbers would be both the type associated with all the properties represented by its nonarbitrary subclasses and also the type associated with the property of being a prime number itself. Hence, although a false sentence such as "1739 is a prime number" is not at present a type crossing, as far as the subject matter approach is concerned, it might very well become a type crossing in the future; and it *would* become a type crossing if the class of prime numbers (as a result of new discoveries) should ever become a subject matter. It is clear, then, that the subject matter approach makes the concept of a type and the concept of a type crossing time-dependent. Yet, such a result, I should think, runs counter to our basic intuitions with respect to those concepts. We do not want to admit the possibility of "1739 is a prime number" being a type crossing, no matter what the circumstances might be, and no matter whether the time be past, present, or distant future. For this reason, the subject matter approach must be regarded to be unacceptable as a theory of type crossings.

Closely related to this fundamental objection to the subject matter approach is the objection that it does not adequately account for the necessary falsity (or conceptual meaninglessness) of essential type crossings. We want to say that "Socrates is a prime number" is a necessary falsehood because its negation can be *proven* from a priori truths alone (in the manner indicated back on page 24). But it cannot be a necessary falsehood so long as its status as a type crossing is accidental or time-dependent. For then the possibility would arise that at some time, past or future, it would not be a type crossing at all, but something else, in which case it could not be regarded as being *necessarily* false. For this reason, it seems clear that the subject matter approach is inadequate. Some other concept than that of subject matter must be found on which to base a theory of essential type crossings. It must be a concept which is *not* time-dependent, for only such a concept could guarantee the necessary falsity of essential type crossings.

It is important to see that the appeal to type-rules or linguistic conventions will not help us here. To bring this out, I shall state the difficulty in terms of three pairs of sentences:

(a)   The concept of truth is a symmetrical relation.
(a') Temporal precedence is a symmetrical relation.

(b)   The concept of truth is a valid argument form.
(b') "q, p⊃q, ∴ p" is a valid argument form.

(c)   The concept of truth is a prime number.
(c') 4 is a prime number.

The first member of each pair is an essential type crossing, whereas the second member is an a priori falsehood which is not a type crossing but which ascribes the same essential property as the first member. The question may be put this way: what is the basis of the distinction between the two sentences in each pair? What makes one a type crossing and not the other? What determines the type associated with the given property in each case? Why, for example, do we regard the type associated with the property of being a symmetrical relation to be the class of relations? Why not take it to be the class of symmetrical relations itself (in which case (a') would be a type crossing) or the class of abstract entities (in which case (a) would not be a type crossing)?

I want to point out that the appeal to type-rules or linguistic conventions does not help us here. It is no good to say simply

that the three type crossings, (a)–(c), violate linguistic conventions, for that might also be said of some (and perhaps all)
of the non-type-crossings. Nor is it any good to say that the type
crossings violate type-rules, for the question arises: what is the
criterion for whether or not a sentence violates type-rules? It is
clear that there is *no* criterion, apart from whatever criterion is
appealed to in order to determine whether or not a given sentence
is a type crossing. And this is true whether type-rules are regarded
as grammatical rules or not. As was pointed out back on page 73,
there can be no evidence that a given sentence violates type-rules
apart from the evidence that it is a type crossing. To define type
crossings as 'sentences which violate type-rules' must ultimately
be circular. Thus, the appeal to type-rules gains us nothing.

What, then, is the basis of the distinction between essential
type crossings and other a priori falsehoods which ascribe essential properties? The thinkability approach offers no solution. The
subject matter approach offers no solution. The linguistic approach offers no solution. As a final stab, let us now consider a
fourth approach, which I shall call the "genus approach".

The genus approach is based on the observation that all essential properties, except for certain ones to be specified, are constructed out of a genus and difference classification. For example,
the property of being a symmetrical relation is constructed out
of being a relation (genus) and being symmetrical (difference).
The property of being a valid argument is constructed out of
being an argument (genus) and being valid (difference). And the
property of being a prime number is constructed out of being a
number (genus) and being prime (difference). In each case, the
genus is the type associated with the given property. For example,
the class of relations is the type associated with the property of
being a symmetrical relation. The class of arguments is the type
associated with the property of being a valid argument. And finally, the class of numbers is the type associated with the property
of being a prime number.[12] Thus, the following definition is sug-

---

[12] It may be objected that the type associated with being a prime number
should be the class of natural numbers, not the general class of numbers

gested: the type associated with an essential property is the genus out of which it is constructed. But there are also essential properties which are represented by just a single concept, e.g., being a relation, being an argument, being a number, and so on. In these cases, it is the single concept which corresponds to the type associated with the property. Thus, such properties are type properties. The type associated with them is the class which they themselves mark off.[13] We may now reformulate the definition as follows:

D_1: The type associated with an essential property which is constructed out of a genus and difference classification (which may be presented by means of the difference alone) is the genus out of which it is constructed.

D_2: The type associated with an essential property which is represented by a single class concept (which is not an abbreviation for a genus and difference classification) is that class which represents the given property.

---

itself. But it has already been shown that several difficulties and counterintuitive results follow from this standpoint (which was originally a standpoint foisted upon us by the subject matter approach). For this reason, it seems preferable to abandon it. On the other hand, if mathematically inclined people want to insist that sentences such as "3i is a prime number" should be regarded as type crossings, then I would suggest to them that the term 'number' as it appears in the expression 'prime number' be taken to mean 'natural number' or 'integer'. I see no reason to deny that this is in fact how mathematicians do take it. It would then follow that the genus out of which the property of being a prime number is constructed is the class of natural numbers (or integers), which, according to our genus approach, would then be the type associated with that property. This, then, provides an alternative solution to the difficulty in question.

[13] It may be objected that sometimes the part of the property corresponding to the *difference* (as opposed to the genus) stands alone, and is thus represented by a single concept, as for example, in the case of being symmetrical, being valid, being prime, etc. However, this does not constitute an exception, because in all such cases the genus is understood. When we say "x is symmetrical" (in the relevant sense), we mean "x is a symmetrical relation". When we say "x is valid" (in the relevant sense), we mean "x is a valid argument". Thus, the property is not really represented by a single concept but rather by an *abbreviation* for a genus and difference classification.

To complete our theory, as given by D_1 and D_2, all we need is the statement of closure: *all* essential properties are either constructed out of genus and difference classifications or else are represented by single class concepts. Thus, if the theory is correct, then D_1 and D_2 cover all essential properties.

The theory works well for a large number of essential properties. Nevertheless, there may be exceptions to it. For example, consider the following sentences:

(74) The figure formed by two obtuse triangles which have a common side is an equilateral rectangle.
(75) The figure formed by two scalene triangles which have a common side is a square.

It might be argued that, since the property of being an equilateral rectangle is an essential property, it would turn out, by D_1, that the type associated with it is the class of rectangles. And since the subject of sentence (74) does not designate a member of that class, (74) would turn out to be a type crossing, which is a counter-intuitive result. Similarly, since the property of being a square is an essential property, it would turn out, by D_2, that it is a type property, so that any sentence ascribing it falsely would be a type crossing. Since sentence (75) does ascribe the property falsely, (75) would turn out to be a type crossing, another counter-intuitive result. However, these alleged counter-examples could be rejected on the grounds that the properties of being an equilateral rectangle and being a square are really not essential properties after all. In order for them to be essential properties, every ascription of them must be a priori. But this condition is not met. Whether or not a given figure has one of the properties in question could be an empirical matter. (Consider, for example, the application of these properties in engineering.) Certainly, it makes sense to speak of something (e.g., a shadow) being a square at one time but not at another time. Thus, the alleged counter-examples are not really counter-examples at all.

However, genuine counter-examples can indeed be constructed

if we go over to relational properties. For example, the arithmetical relations 'is greater than', 'is divisible by', 'is the square root of' are essential (relational) properties which are neither constructed out of genus and difference classifications nor represented by single class concepts. Thus, the statement of closure is shown to be false.[14] We can present the counter-example by means of the following sentence pair:

(d)   The concept of truth is the square root of chemistry.
(d') The number 3 is the square root of the number 6.

What makes (d) a type crossing, but not (d')? Clearly, the genus approach will not help us here. Other counter-examples of this same sort may be found in the area of logical relations, such as deducibility and class inclusion. Consider the following pair:

(e)   The concept of truth entails chemistry.
(e') The proposition that grass is green entails the proposition that if grass is green then snow is white.

Whereas (e) is a type crossing, (e') is an a priori falsehood which is not a type crossing but which ascribes the same essential (relational) property as (e). It is clear that the difference between the two sentences cannot be accounted for by means of the genus approach.

Let us now consider a separate theory which may be applied to essential relations. Any essential relation, R, can be adequately defined according to this pattern: "R (definiendum) is the relation between two x's that obtains when one of the x's bears relation S (definiens) to the other x". When such a definition is given, the type associated with R invariably turns out to be the class of pairs of x's. Examples of definitions following this pattern are the following:

---

[14]   One may wish to maintain that the relations in question *are* represented by single class concepts (involving classes of pairs). But this will do no good as far as the genus approach is concerned, for it would follow that any sentence which ascribes the relations falsely would be a type crossing. Clearly, however, this is not the case, as may be seen by appeal to such sentences as "4 is greater than 5", "22 is divisible by 3", and so on.

"Being the square root of" is the relation between two numbers that obtains when the second number is the product of the first number and itself (the first number).

Entailment is the relation between two propositions that obtains when the second proposition must be true given the truth of the first proposition.

By applying the theory to these definitions, we get the result that the type associated with the relation of "being the square root of" is the class of pairs of numbers. And the type associated with the relation of entailment is the class of pairs of propositions. Both of these results are in agreement with our intuitions on the matter. I shall refer to the theory presented here as the "definition approach", and I shall defend it as an adequate theory of essential relations.

The objection that immediately comes to mind in connection with the definition approach is that it is *ad hoc*. After all, it may be asked, how are we to determine the correct way to formulate the definition of a given relation according to the required pattern? In order to formulate the definition in the right way, the class of x's which we choose must indeed be the type of pairs associated with the given relation. So we are going in a circle. We define the type associated with the relation in terms of a definition, but in order to formulate the definition correctly we must already know the type associated with the relation.

The circle can be broken, however, if the criterion for correct formulation of the definition does not make any appeal to the type associated with the given relation. And this can indeed be brought about by the following consideration: people do not have any difficulty in formulating definitions of the required sort; people agree on what the definition should be in each case. This, then, is the criterion for formulating definitions of the required sort: simply appeal to how people would normally do it. In whatever way people would normally formulate such definitions, that is to be considered the right way. The point of the definition approach, then, is that the class of x's to which people would normally appeal in formulating a definition of the required sort invariably turns out to be the type associated with the given relation. Thus, the way to discover that type is to determine the definition in question.

It may be objected that we could just as well define the type associated with a given relation as the type people *normally associate with* that relation, and thereby dispense with the appeal to definitions altogether. In fact, this could be applied to all properties, not just to relations. The reason this would not work, however, is that the concept of the *type* associated with a relation (or property) is a technical concept, and so the question cannot arise as to what people would *normally* take to be that type. On the other hand, the concept of the *definition* of a relation is not a technical concept, and so the question *can* arise as to what people would normally take to be that definition. In the definition approach, a technical concept (type) is being defined in terms of a non-technical concept (definition), which seems, after all, quite sensible. As for the question whether the definition approach could be revised so as to apply to non-relational properties, I shall point out that this is precisely what is being done in the genus approach. The genus approach is a special revised form of the definition approach, formulated with particular reference to non-relational essential properties. At any rate, the genus approach will be applied to non-relational essential properties, and the definition approach will be applied to relational essential properties. And I shall refer to this combination as the "genus-definition" approach to essential type crossings.

One question which naturally arises at this point is whether the genus-definition approach can stand up to the objection about time-dependence, which proved so crushing to the subject matter approach. Certainly the genus approach does not involve time-dependence, for the genus out of which an essential property is constructed cannot vary from time to time. As an illustration, the genus out of which the property of being a symmetrical relation is constructed is the class of relations. But it makes no sense to suggest that this class could change so that the genus would at some other time be a different class. Obviously, if the genus were no longer the class of relations, then the property in question would no longer be the property of being a symmetrical relation. Similarly, if a property is represented by a single class concept, then it could not, at a different time, be represented by a different class concept and still be the same property. I conclude, then, that the genus approach does not in any way involve time-dependence.

But what about the definition approach? Surely what is and what is not an adequate definition of a word can change from one time to another. This is true, but in the definition approach it is not a word that is being defined, but a relational property. That is, the definition provides an analysis of a *concept,* not a stipulated or reported equivalent for a linguistic expression. I shall maintain that it is impossible to formulate two definitions of a given relation which meet all of the following conditions: (1) they are both of the required form (i.e., "R is the relation between two x's that obtains when one of the x's bears relation S to the other x"), (2) they both adequately define the given relation, and (3) the classes of x's to which they appeal are different. If I am right, and it is impossible to formulate two definitions (perhaps somehow separated by time) which meet all three conditions, then it follows that the fact that a certain type is associated with a given relation according to the definition approach is an essential property of that relation, and, hence, is in no way time-dependent. Thus, the genus-definition approach is not open to the objection having to do with time-dependence. As a result, it is a theory which adequately accounts for the necessary falsity (or conceptual meaninglessness) of essential type crossings.

What is needed now is an explanation of the rationale behind the genus-definition approach. Why is it, we want to know, that the key concept in understanding accidental type crossings is that of thinkability, whereas the key concepts in understanding essential type crossings are those of genus and definition? I think the answer lies in the fact that accidental properties are properties the application of which is ascertained by experience, whereas essential properties are not. On the contrary, essential properties are, so to speak, creatures of definition. They are abstract concepts that are not in any way related to sense perception, but are brought into being by the juxtaposition of various abstractions (or by the division of certain very general classes) by means of genus and difference definitions. That is why they should be amenable to the genus-definition approach. On the other hand, the applicability of accidental properties in given cases can be ascertained only by appeal to possible experience. And the test for what experiences are possible or are not possible is the thinkability test, which is really an appeal to imagination. This latter point will be taken up in Chapter 7.

Let us now raise the question whether there is any possibility that the genus-definition approach could be applied to accidental properties (in which case there would be no need to appeal to the thinkability test). I believe the answer is "no". Unlike essential properties, accidental properties are, for the most part, neither constructed out of genus and difference classifications nor are they type properties. Color properties provide a simple illustration. There are just too many counter-examples for the genus approach to gain any foothold in the area of accidental properties. I attribute this to the considerations mentioned above. The genus approach will work only for concepts which are brought into being by the division of certain very general classes (types) by means of genus and difference definitions. Since accidental properties are not brought into being in that way, the genus approach will not work for them.

What, then, about the definition approach? Can it be extended to the area of accidental relations? Admittedly, it would work for some accidental relations (e.g., 'is the cousin of', 'weighs more than'). But there are many for which it would not work, especially those relations which are simple and unanalyzable, such as 'is darker than', 'is louder than', etc. I conclude, then, that the definition approach is not generally applicable to the area of accidental relations. Rather, each approach has its own realm of application. The thinkability approach is applicable to accidental properties but not to essential properties. The genus approach is applicable to non-relational essential properties, but not to relational essential properties or to accidental properties. And finally, the definition approach is applicable to relational essential properties, but not (as it is given) to non-relational essential properties or to accidental properties (though it could work for *some* accidental relational properties).

The question might be raised as to how a non-type-crossing is to be excluded from the class of type crossings by the general theory presented here. Consider, for example, our sentences (14) –(16). Sentence (14) is excluded from the class of essential type crossings because the property it ascribes is not an essential property; it is excluded from the class of accidental type crossings by the considerations raised on page 112. Sentence (15) is excluded from the class of accidental type crossings because the property it ascribes is not an accidental property; and it is excluded from the class of essential type crossings by the considerations raised on pages 125–126. Sentence (16), which has not been discussed as yet, could be analyzed as a relational sentence which ascribes the accidental relational property of "—— moving in a direction perpendicular to each of three adjacent edges of —— at the same time" to the ordered set: an object, a cube. Presumably the type associated with that property would be the class of ordered pairs the first member of which is a physical thing and the second member of which is a solid object. But, then, the ordered set in question *would* be a member of that type. Hence, sentence (16) would not be a simple type crossing at all.[15] Thus,

15 In order to determine whether or not (16) is a complex type crossing, we need to analyze it by appeal to the language of symbolic logic. When analyzed, it would read somewhat as follows: There exist a t, u, v, w, x, y, and z such that: t is a time; u is an object; v is a cube; w is a direction; u is moving in w; x, y, and z are edges of v; x, y, and z are adjacent to one another; and finally, w is perpendicular to x at t; w is perpendicular to y at t; and w is perpendicular to z at t. Application of our definition of simple type crossings to each of the individual clauses of this compound sentence reveals that none of them is a type crossing. Nor are "type incompatible" predicates applied anywhere in it to any one variable. Hence, sentence (16) is in no way a complex type crossing.

we have developed a theory which clearly excludes sentences (14)–(16) from the class of type crossings, which was one of our main objectives. This discussion (together with the passages referred back to) can be used as a model illustrating how non-type-crossings are to be excluded from the class of type crossings by means of our theory.

I must admit that I have more confidence in the thinkability approach than in the genus-definition approach. As it stands, the genus-definition approach is quite sketchy and incomplete. No doubt, confrontation with potential counter-examples will either refute it or else mold it into something more precise and more complete. Which of these roads the theory will take must be left to the future to decide. All I can say is that if the genus-definition approach to essential type crossings goes down to defeat, as did its predecessors, then I just do not know what could possibly replace it. The problem of essential type crossings would in that case be a fundamental mystery – an unsolved problem in the border area of linguistics and philosophy.

One final note: in the present section I have been concerned with the concept of "the type associated with a given property". One might wonder what there is to be said about the concept of a type itself. In the narrow sense, a type (or category) is no more than a class of things associated with some property or other. In the broad sense, which is the sense in which Ryle uses the term, a type (or category) is a class of propositional factors associated with some propositional form or other. (See the quotation from Ryle on page 76, above.) I agree with Ryle that there are not just ten types, as Aristotle said, or twelve types, as Kant maintained, but an indefinite number. But I am not convinced that Ryle is using the word 'type' in the same sense as Aristotle or Kant, despite his remarks in the article "Categories". In my sense of 'type', at any rate, one can meaningfully speak of a "type of thing" and "a thing belonging to (or being a member of) a type". But it is not at all clear whether this would make sense in Aristotle's or Kant's terminology (in which examples of types would be given by such terms as 'substance', 'quantity', 'quality', 'causality', etc.). For this reason, the present section is not intended to throw any new light on the topic of "categories" as conceived by Aristotle or Kant. Its only purpose is to provide the foundation for what may someday become a satisfactory theory of type crossings.

6.4. SUMMARY OF RESULTS

After such an extended discussion of the problems confronting a definition of 'type crossing', perhaps some sort of recapitulation is in order. Our original working definition of a type crossing was that of a sentence which says of one type of thing something that has application only to a different type of thing. Our problem in the present chapter was to replace this working definition by something more precise, and to do this without running up against the difficulties inherent in the theories discussed in Chapter 5. All this is supposed to be accomplished by our basic formulation, the final version of which is expressed as follows:

A simple type crossing is a sentence which ascribes in a positive manner to a specific thing (or set of things), x, a property the type associated with which is a class to which x does not belong.

This formula can be understood in terms of the following subordinate definitions:

(a) A sentence ascribes a property *in a positive manner* if and only if it is not of the form "S is not P" or equivalent to any sentence of that form. (With respect to the form "S is not P", see footnotes 4 and 5.)
(b) A *specific* thing is anything which does not include within it things of many different types.
(c) The notion of "ascribing a property to a set of things" is to be understood to mean relating things by means of a relation.

In addition to replacing our working definition of a type crossing by something more precise, we also attempted to develop a theory applicable to sentences which involve a crossing of types, but which, because of their complex structure, do not conform to the working definition. We referred to these as "complex type crossings" and put forward the following definition:

A complex type crossing is a sentence whose translation into the language of symbolic logic applies predicates to a variable in a negation-free context which designate properties at least one of which has associated with it a type none of whose members has the other property.

It was noted that the topic of complex type crossings is not directly related to the main problem of the chapter.

Both the definition of 'simple type crossing' and the definition of 'complex type crossing' make use of the concept of the type associated with a given property. For the purpose of explicating this quite fundamental concept, properties were divided into accidental properties and essential properties (see page 113). Then the following definitions were finally presented:

The type associated with an accidental property is the class of things (or class of sets of things) which can thinkably have that property.

The type associated with a non-relational essential property which is constructed out of a genus and difference classification is the genus out of which it is constructed.

The type associated with a non-relational essential property which is represented by a single class concept (which is not an abbreviation for a genus and difference classification) is that class which represents the given property.

(All non-relational essential properties are either constructed out of genus and difference classifications or else represented by single class concepts.)

The type associated with a relational essential property is the class of pairs of things to which an appeal is normally made when one defines the relation according to the following pattern: "R (definiendum) is the relation between two things that obtains when one of the things bears relation S (definiens) to the other thing." (Although this applies to just 2-placed relations, it is assumed that it can, with only minor alterations, be extended to cover "higher placed" relations as well.)

Of these four definitions, the last three are considered to be all part of the "genus-definition" approach to essential properties (or essential type crossings).

Although I have some doubts about the adequacy of the genus-definition approach as it is formulated here, I feel that whatever difficulties there may be can be handled through alterations within the theory, and that they do not necessitate scrapping the theory altogether. Indeed, if either the thinkability approach or the genus-definition approach had to be abandoned, then I have no idea what could possibly replace it.

UNTHINKABILITY

7.1. THE PHILOSOPHICAL PROBLEM REVISITED

At the end of Chapter 3, it was said that, given certain conditions, the problem of defining 'type crossing' could be a problem for linguistics. In contrast, the problem of why type crossings are meaningless is a strictly philosophical problem. We discussed it in Chapters 3 and 4, but only in a negative way – to show that the answer "type crossings are meaningless because they violate conventions of language" is incorrect. The answer that I shall want to expound and defend in the present chapter is that type crossings are meaningless because they designate unthinkable propositions.

Note that I am applying the adjective 'unthinkable' to what I call "propositions", but it should be pointed out that my use of the term 'proposition' is somewhat broader than that of many other writers in the field. I want to speak of propositions as being expressed by *any* declarative sentences at all, even those which are meaningless. A proposition is to be thought of as any combination of ideas or concepts expressed in declarative form. For example, *that the theory of relatively is blue* is the proposition expressed by the sentence "the theory of relativity is blue" (as well as the sentence "die Relativitätstheorie ist blau"), and it is, indeed, an unthinkable proposition.

It might be objected that unthinkability could not be the basis of the meaninglessness of type crossings because there are many sentences other than type crossings which also designate unthinkable propositions. For example, sentences (14)–(16) are in this category, as well as all self-contradictory sentences. In reply to this objection, I shall argue that such sentences are

meaningless in the same sense in which type crossings are meaningless, and the basis of their meaninglessness is the same as
that in the case of type crossings.

Of course, one may want to *stipulate* a sense of 'meaningless'
in which, say, "Socrates is a prime number" is meaningless, but
"the number 4 is a prime number" is not meaningless. I cannot
deny that. But what it would come to, ultimately, is that 'being
meaningless', in this sense, is equivalent to 'being a type crossing'. In other words, this sense of 'meaningless' would be
definable only in terms of the concept of a type crossing, so that
the basis of the meaninglessness of type crossings would be
nothing more than the fact that they *are type crossings*. The
question "why are type crossings meaningless?" would be re-
ducible to the question "why are type crossings type crossings?"
or, in other words, "what is a type crossing?" Let us distinguish
this sense of 'meaningless' from all others by referring to it as
"type meaninglessness". Thus, the question "what is the basis of
the *type meaninglessness* of type crossings?" can be shown to
come to no more than the question "what is a type crossing?",
which we have already discussed at great length in Chapter 6.

There is another sense of 'meaningless', which I have referred
to as "conceptual meaninglessness", according to which a sentence is meaningless if and only if we cannot understand what it
would be like for it to be true. It is in this sense of 'meaningless'
that most, if not all, necessary falsehoods are meaningless (including type crossings as well as other sorts of necessary falsehoods). And it is with respect to this sense of 'meaningless' that
the question is raised: what is the basis of the meaninglessness of
type crossings? My answer is that the basis of the conceptual
meaninglessness of type crossings is the same as that of other
necessary falsehoods, namely the unthinkability of the proposition expressed by the sentence. This view is put forward in opposition to the more fashionable view (which was attacked in Chapters 3 and 4) that the basis of the conceptual meaninglessness of
type crossings and other necessary falsehoods lies in their violation of linguistic rules or conventions. It will be my purpose in the

present chapter to attempt to defend the appeal to unthinkability against the most important objections to it.

But before embarking on this task, I shall first take up two preliminary objections. When I say that the basis of the meaning-lessness of type crossings lies in the concept of unthinkability, I am presupposing two things. I am presupposing that type cross-ings *are* meaningless, and also that it makes sense to raise the question as to *why* they are meaningless. A philosopher may want to reject one of these presuppositions. So, it is important to show that, in doing so, he would be making a mistake.

Consider, first of all, this argument. The purpose of language is to communicate, and the purpose of the term 'meaningless' is to signify that an attempt at communication has failed. But then type crossings can never properly be said to be meaningless, for they are never used in attempts at communication. The very interpretation given to the individual words in a type crossing precludes such a sentence from ever being used for purposes of communication. The question could never arise for such a sen-tence whether communication by means of it was successful or unsuccessful. Thus, type crossings cannot properly be said to be meaningful or meaningless, and hence, the question of the basis of the *meaninglessness* of type crossings must be an im-proper question. Type crossings are simply not a part of language at all.

My reply to this objection is that it comes to nothing. Even if one refuses to call type crossings meaningless, he must at least admit that they are *different* from ordinary sentences, that there is *some* distinction to be drawn between them and the sen-tences uttered in everyday life. So the question can still be raised: what is the ultimate basis of that distinction? The difference between this question and what I have called "the philosophical problem of the basis of the meaninglessness of type crossings" is no more than a terminological difference, and therefore not worth bothering about.

The second preliminary objection is that the question *why* type crossings are meaningless is simply an unanswerable question. It is like asking why cutting one's fingernails is painless in a sense of 'why' which does not call for a physiological explanation. After all, it is in principle possible to give a physiological explanation for why type crossings are meaningless – in terms of auditory and visual nerve impulses, subsequent brain processes (or lack of them), and motor responses. Yet, it is clear that this is not what is wanted when it is asked *why* type crossings are meaningless.

The term 'why' is being used in a way which makes such an answer irrelevant. Suppose, then, that the term 'why' were being used in that same way in the question "why is cutting one's fingernails painless?" It seems we would simply have to reply that the question is unanswerable. In the same way, according to the objection, there simply is no answer to the question "why are type crossings meaningless?" (once a physiological explanation is ruled out as being irrelevant). All we can say is that cutting one's fingernails is painless because we feel no pain from it, or that type crossings are meaningless because we do not mean anything by them, which, of course, is to say *nothing*. Thus, the question regarding the basis of the meaninglessness of type crossings must be taken to be an unanswerable question.

My reply to this objection is that the question cannot be unanswerable, for I have answered it. My answer still needs to be defended further, but if that defense is successful, then it will in itself constitute an adequate reply to this second preliminary objection. Of course, if it is unsuccessful, then we ought to come back and reconsider this objection as perhaps expressing the truth about the matter.

My appeal to the concept of unthinkability (or thinkability) is twofold. I appeal to it in order to answer both of these questions:

(1) What is the basis of the type meaninglessness of accidental type crossings?

(2) What is the basis of the conceptual meaninglessness of all type crossings?

Question (1) is answered as follows:

Accidental type crossings are type meaningless because they ascribe in a positive manner to a specific thing (or set of things), x, an accidental property such that the type of specific thing (or type of set of things) which can *thinkably* have that property is a class to which x does not belong. (This also constitutes a definition of 'accidental type crossing'.)

Question (2) is answered as follows:

Type crossings are conceptually meaningless because they designate *unthinkable* propositions (i.e., combinations of concepts which cannot be put together in thought).

It is acknowledged that certain sentences other than type crossings may also be conceptually meaningless (and be conceptually meaningless for the same reason as in the case of type crossings). This matter will be discussed more fully in Chapter 8.

There are three main objections to the appeal to unthinkability. The first is that the term 'unthinkable', as it is used here, does not make sense, for it cannot be clearly defined. The second objection is that unthinkability is a subjective or relative concept, since what is unthinkable for one person may not be unthinkable for someone else. Hence, it cannot constitute the basis for understanding the nature of type crossings, for the property of being a type crossing is objective, not subjective. The third objection is that the concept of unthinkability is vague, for there are many propositions that constitute borderline cases between the thinkable and the unthinkable. This, then, would infect the theory of type crossings under consideration and make that vague as well. In the next three sections of the present chapter, I shall take up these objections individually and try to defend the appeal to unthinkability against them.

7.2. THE PROBLEM OF DEFINITION

In answer to the question "what is unthinkability?", I shall say, very briefly, that it is the inability to be thought or to be conceived; or, in other words, it is conceptual impossibility. This immediately distinguishes the sense in which I use the term 'unthinkable' from its most common meaning in ordinary language, which is 'out of the question' or 'not to be considered'. In ordinary language it would be true to say, "It is unthinkable for the President to beat his wife in public", but in my sense of 'unthinkable', this would be false. Whereas, in ordinary language, the term 'unthinkable' is used mainly as an emphatic device for expressing strong disbelief or disapproval about some matter of fact, in the technical sense in which I am using the term, it cannot be truly applied to matters of fact, only to necessary falsehoods.

It is possible to partly indicate the meaning of 'unthinkable' through the use of examples. Here is a simplified list which may be taken as an ostensive definition of the expression 'unthinkable proposition':

Thinkable propositions

1. The blood of a squirrel is blue.
2. The President will beat his wife in public.
3. Two gallons of alcohol added to two gallons of water result in four gallons of mixture.
4. Some bachelors are 1000 years old.
5. Some red objects emit only light having the wave length which corresponds to green.

Unthinkable propositions

1'. The theory of relativity is blue.
2'. The President will drink his wife in public.
3'. Two plus two equals three.

4'. Some bachelors are married.
5'. Some red objects are all green.

This ostensive definition of 'unthinkable proposition' is useful only for giving a rough indication of what the expression means.[1]

---

[1] The reason why no true propositions appear in the list is that the question of whether a proposition is thinkable or unthinkable does not normally arise in the case of true propositions. The distinction is applied only to

It would be of no use in explaining the meaning of the expression to one, say, who interprets a priori falsity in terms of the violation of linguistic conventions, for he would not be able to distinguish the meaning of 'p is unthinkable' from 'S violates linguistic conventions', where S is the sentence which designates proposition p. In other words, given the ostensive definition alone, he might come to the conclusion that 'unthinkable proposition' means 'proposition which is designated by a sentence which violates linguistic conventions', which is not at all what I intend it to mean. Therefore, an ostensive definition cannot by itself be considered an adequate explanation of the concept of unthinkability. It seems that an appeal must also be made to some such definition as this: a proposition is unthinkable if and only if no one is able to think it. And the *test* for whether or not a proposition is thinkable by anyone is simply to try to think it.

Now the crucial question becomes: what is it to "think a proposition"? The expression itself seems awkward, for one does not normally use the verb 'to think' in such a way that it takes a direct object. I admit that there is a departure from ordinary usage here, but it is quite unavoidable. Ordinary usage does not provide any alternative expression that would serve my purpose.[2]

It may be said that to think a proposition is to *imagine* what it would be like for the proposition to be true. But then a distinction needs to be drawn between two kinds of imagining. I shall refer to these as quantitative imagining and qualitative imagining. To imagine quantitatively is to call up a mental image which corresponds in every quantitative detail to the object of which it is supposed to be an image. Qualitative imagining, on the other hand, applies mainly to propositions, rather than to objects, and

---

false propositions, because it would be completely trivial to say of a true proposition that it is thinkable.

[2]   This same point is made by G. E. M. Anscombe in her book *An Introduction to Wittgenstein's Tractatus* (London, Hutchinson University Library, 1959), p. 69n. She says of Wittgenstein's use of the verb 'to think' (as in 'to think the sense of the picture') that it is "a Germanism which it seems necessary to retain in English".

does not require the calling up of any precise images. To bring this out by means of an example, consider these two requests:

(76) Imagine a 23-sided polygon.
(77) Imagine what it would be like for a polygon to have 23 sides.

I suspect that there may be some inclination to say that the task involved here is an impossible one, especially in the case of (76). The average person is not able to call up an image of a 23-sided polygon which is so quantitatively accurate that it is distinguishable from an image of a 22-sided polygon or a 25-sided polygon. Whereas most of us can distinguish an image of a 5-sided figure from that of a 6-sided figure, we cannot do this when the number of sides is considerably increased. Let us refer to the sense of 'imagine' in which (76) represents an impossible task (or at least one which is too difficult to accomplish without much practice) as "quantitative imagining".

There is another sense of 'imagining', which I shall call "qualitative imagining", in which we can perfectly well carry out the task called for in (77). We are inclined to say that we can imagine what it is like for a polygon to have 23 sides, for we can imagine what it would be like to count the sides of a figure and arrive at the number 23. All that is involved in qualitative imagining is either contemplating the co-occurrence of certain properties or else contemplating the process of verifying a given proposition. Consider, for example, the sentence "all crows are black". This sentence designates a proposition which is qualitatively imaginable, but not quantitatively imaginable. It is qualitatively imaginable because we can contemplate or imagine the co-occurrence of the two properties: being a crow and being black. But it is not quantitatively imaginable because we cannot call up a mental image which depicts *all crows* in precise quantitative detail. In general, if our inability to imagine a proposition is due to some large quantity referred to in it, so that by reducing that quantity the proposition becomes imaginable, then the proposition is only quantitatively unimaginable, not qualitatively unimaginable. On the other hand, if our inability to imagine a proposition is due to our inability to contemplate the co-occurrence of two properties or to contemplate the process by which the proposition might be verified, then the unimaginability is qualitative rather than quantitative. For example, with respect to the sentence "chemistry has 23 vertices", the proposition which is designated is qualitatively (not quantitatively) unimaginable, for the proposition would remain unimaginable even if the quantity referred to in it were to be reduced.

We may now define "thinking a proposition" as *qualitatively* imagining what it would be like for it to be true. This does not require the calling up of any quantitatively precise mental images. All it requires is either contemplating the co-occurrence of the properties contained in the proposition (as in the case of the sentence "all crows are black") or else contemplating the process of verifying the proposition (as in the case of the sentence "that figure has 23 sides"). It seems to me that only necessary falsehoods could ever fail such a test and thereby be classified as "unthinkable".

We have identified thinking a given proposition with doing either of the following: contemplating the co-occurrence of the properties contained in the proposition or contemplating what it would be like to verify the proposition. But it is clear that this does not provide any *analysis* of "thinking a proposition". After all, the word 'contemplate' is not in any way simpler than the word 'think'; nor are there any other words in terms of which the sentence "x thinks p" (where 'x' represents a person and 'p' represents a proposition) can be analyzed. It seems that such a sentence is logically simple and cannot be analyzed or reduced to still simpler terms.

Consider the following sentence, which I claim to be unanalyzable:

(78) Jones is thinking the proposition that water boils at room temperature.

Let us compare (78) with two other sentences, which are also unanalyzable, namely:

(79) That hat is red.
(80) Jones has a pain.

The similarities between (78) and (80) are greater than those between (78) and (79). Sentence (79) is not like the other two because it is not a relational sentence. But the main difference is that it can be both publicly and conclusively verified, whereas (78) and (80) cannot (at least not at the same time both publicly and conclusively).

There are also differences between (78) and (80), among which are the following:

a) A pain is a concrete entity, having duration, whereas a proposition is a timeless abstract entity. Also, a pain is private (in the sense that no two people can have the same pain), whereas a proposition is public (in the sense that two people *can* think the same proposition).

b) Whereas (80) can be confirmed by Jones's non-linguistic behavior, (78) can only be confirmed by what Jones tells us.

c) The most important difference is that whereas the expression 'having a pain' has a standard use in ordinary language, the expression 'thinking a proposition' is not an expression of ordinary language at all; rather, it is a technical term of epistemology which does not even have a standard use among philosophers. It is mainly this fact which makes the problem of definition such a difficult one. The upshot of the present discussion, then, is that even among other unanalyzable concepts, there are none which are very much like the concept of "thinking a proposition". And this, of course, makes the task of explaining that concept extremely difficult.

Another factor which sets the concept apart is that it appears to be the most basic of all epistemological concepts. Just as believing is more basic than knowing (in the sense that it is a necessary condition for the latter, but not a sufficient condition), so also thinking (in the relevant sense) is more basic than believing, for it is certainly possible to think a proposition without believing it. But whether it is possible to believe a proposition without thinking it is indeed a debatable point. My own answer is to say that it is *not* possible, but I shall not defend that view here; it would require a thorough investigation of the concept of belief, which would take us too far from the topic.

Instead of attempting to analyze what cannot be analyzed, it would be more profitable to try to explain the meaning of "thinking a proposition" in terms of a model. One model that will *not* do for this purpose is that of a person posed in the manner of Rodin's statue "The Thinker", while gears and wheels turn about inside his head. This tends to associate "thinking" with problem-solving, whereas "thinking a proposition" does not involve problem-solving at all. Rather, it is something immediate and intuitive, not requiring time or concentration in any way. The model that I shall put forward is the familiar one of placing pegs into holes in boards. Thus, it may be said that thinking a proposition is like putting a peg into a hole in a board. Failing to think a proposition because it is unthinkable is like failing to put a peg into a hole because it does not fit. The unthinkability of a proposition is like the inability of a peg to fit into a given hole.[3] Or, to coin a new term, it is like the "unfittability" of a peg with respect to a given hole.

In this model, the pegs represent the things which sentences are about (i.e., the things designated by their subjects). The holes represent the properties which are ascribed to those things. And the board itself could be taken to represent the grammatical form of the sentence. Thus, just as pegs come in all shapes and sizes, so also things are of many different *types*. And just as pegs are sometimes not of the right shape or size to fit into a given hole, so also things are sometimes not of the right type to have the properties ascribed to them in propositions.

Consider some particular examples. The sentence "the theory of relativity is blue" can be said to be like trying to put a square peg into a round hole. Then the sequence "the theory of relativ-

---

[3] Note that the analogy is with pegs fitting *into* holes. Thus, it does not have to be a close fit. A small peg and a large hole are to be thought of as satisfying the conditions for "fitting".

ity is but" is like trying to put a peg into a board that has no hole at all. And the sequence "is blue the of theory relativity" is like a group of pegs and boards just lying there without anyone trying to do anything with them. Thus, being grammatical corresponds to someone *trying* to put a peg into a hole in a board. And just as someone could try to put a peg into a hole even though it does not fit into the hole, so also a sentence can be grammatical even though the proposition which it expresses is an unthinkable proposition.

The most important point about this model is its objectivity. That which determines whether or not a peg fits into a hole is the size and shape of the peg and hole, not *who* is attempting to do the fitting. Similarly, that which determines whether or not a proposition is thinkable is the nature of the concepts involved, not *who* is attempting to do the thinking. Thus, like the ability of a peg to fit a hole, thinkability is an objective concept. This is a point which I shall defend at length in the next section.

I shall now recapitulate. In reply to the question "what is unthinkability?", the following five points may be made:

1. It is possible to give an ostensive definition of the expression 'unthinkable proposition' by giving examples of propositions which are unthinkable and propositions which are not unthinkable.

2. Unthinkability can be contextually defined as follows: "a proposition is unthinkable if and only if no one is able to think it".

3. Thinking a given proposition may be identified with qualitatively imagining what it would be like for the proposition to be true (i.e., contemplating the co-occurrence of the properties contained in the proposition or else contemplating the process of verifying the proposition). Admittedly, though, this does not constitute an analysis of the concept of "thinking a proposition".

4. The concept of thinking a proposition is logically simple and unanalyzable. Furthermore, it is quite unlike all other concepts which are also simple and unanalyzable.

5. Thinking a proposition is like putting a peg into a hole in

a board. Unthinkability, like the inability of a peg to fit into a hole, is an objective property.

It is true that these five points do not exactly define the concept of unthinkability, nor do they even come close to supplying a complete explanation of it. Yet, there is no other concept than the one I have in mind with respect to which all five points would be true. For this reason, I feel that the question "what is unthinkability?" (and, with it, the first main objection to the appeal to unthinkability) has been adequately answered. In any case, more will be learned about the concept as we move along to new topics.

7.3. SUBJECTIVITY AND OBJECTIVITY

The second main objection to adopting unthinkability as a criterion for whether or not a sentence is a type crossing (or is meaningless) is that it would be a subjective criterion. This objection is based on the following principle:

P: What is unthinkable for one person may not be unthinkable for another.

If we adopted unthinkability as our criterion, then it would follow, by virtue of principle P, that what is a type crossing for one person may not be a type crossing for another This would, of course, be an intolerable conclusion, since no one would then be justified in saying that "the theory of relativity is blue" is a type crossing. A person would be justified only in saying that it is a type crossing *for him* that *he* cannot think it (though perhaps someone else can). The concept of a type crossing would in that case be completely useless and pointless. Clearly, then, I cannot say that the concept of a type crossing is in any way subjective or relative. It seems that what I must do to defend my theory of type crossings against the charge of subjectivity is to show that the principle on which that charge is based (namely, P) is false.

Let us first consider various arguments that may be put forward in favor of P. One of them goes as follows. The test for whether or not a proposition is unthinkable is to try to think it. But wherever people *try* to do something, some will fail and others will succeed. So, whereas some will fail to think a given proposition, others will succeed in thinking it. Therefore, what is unthinkable for one person may not be unthinkable for another.

Now, it is true that some people may succeed in a given task and others fail. But it does not follow that the possibility of doing the task is subjective or relative. Consider, for example, our model of putting pegs into holes. If a person is paralyzed, then he will be unable to put a given peg into a given hole, even though he may try very hard to do it. But it would be absurd to conclude from this that *for him* the peg does not fit the hole. It makes no sense to apply the subjective qualifier 'for so-and-so' in the case of a peg's fitting a hole in a board. We want to say that either the peg fits or it does not fit, that this is a purely objective matter. Yet, the test for whether the peg fits the hole is to *try* to put it into the hole. It will fail to fit if and only if no one is able to put it in. Thus, the fact that the test for whether a peg fits a hole is to *try* to put it into the hole does not make "fittability" a subjective property. Analogously, the fact that the test for whether a proposition is unthinkable is to *try* to think it does not make unthinkability a subjective property.

It might be objected that the analogy breaks down because "fittability" can be defined in terms of *measurements*, whereas unthinkability cannot. In other words, for each size and shape of hole, it is possible to specify, for each shape of peg, the maximum size which would fit into that hole. For example, if we want to fit a peg with a square cross section into a circular hole, then we can appeal to the principles of plane geometry to calculate the maximum length of the sides of the square. Our result is a specification of how small the square must be in order for the peg to fit into the hole. But since unthinkability cannot be defined in terms of measurements, according to the objection, it must be regarded as a subjective concept. However, definability in terms of measurements is certainly not a necessary condition of objectivity. Furthermore, there is a good analogy to measurements in the case of unthinkability. Just as, for each hole, it is possible to specify the size peg that can fit into the hole, so also, for each property, it is possible to specify the type of thing that can *thinkably* have that property. Therefore, the objection mentioned is not successful in weakening the analogy between "fittability" and thinkability.

Another argument in favor of P is that decisions regarding thinkability and unthinkability involve some *mental* process. For example, when I see that it is unthinkable for the theory of relativity to be blue, I must be classifying the theory of relativity as such-and-such a type of thing, different from the type of thing that can have a color, and this classification or distinguishing between types of thing is a mental process of some sort. According to the argument, this constitutes grounds for believing P, because, for any mental process, there are variations among people as regards proficiency in carrying it out. What is unthinkable for one person, therefore, may not be unthinkable for another. And this argument cannot be answered on the basis of any analogy between someone thinking a proposition and someone putting a peg into a hole, for the latter, unlike the former, is a purely *physical* process, and its occurrence can be verified publicly.

However, I believe the argument can be answered with the help of a different analogy. Let us consider the mental process of dividing a number by 3. I am sure that some people are much more proficient in arithmetical calculations than others. One person may be able to see almost immediately that the number 32532 is (evenly) divisible by 3, whereas another might labor for a long time at the calculation and finally come up with the (incorrect) result that the number is not divisible by 3. What would we say when confronted by such divergent results? One thing we would definitely not say is that the number is divisible by 3 for one person but not for the other. It would be absurd to suggest that divisibility by 3 is a subjective property or that whether or not a number is divisible by 3 depends on who is doing the dividing.

When one person says of a number that it is divisible by 3 and another says that it is not divisible by 3, then it seems that there are just three possibilities open: someone has either made a mistake in calculation or else is using his words in a different way from the other or else is just not serious, but is playing a kind of prank. It is this fact – that there are *only* these three possibilities – that makes divisibility by 3 an objective property rather than a subjective property. In other words, although the test for whether or not a number is divisible by 3 is to try to divide it by 3, and although this process of dividing by 3 is a mental process and admits of degrees of proficiency, nevertheless, it would be absurd to say that what is divisible by 3 for one person may not be divisible by 3 for another. I want to claim that unthinkability is, in the same way, an objective property. If one person were to say of a proposition that it is unthinkable and another were to say that it is not unthinkable, I want to argue that there are just three possibilities open: either the two disputants are not really talking about the same proposition or at least one of them is not using the term 'unthinkable' in the relevant sense or else one of them is not to be taken seriously. This fact – that there are *only* these three possibilities – makes unthinkability an objective property of propositions rather than a subjective property. The possibility which is eliminated (or which would be absurd) is that one and the same proposition should be unthinkable for one person but not for another.

At this point, an objection might be raised against the analogy between unthinkability and divisibility by 3. It might be argued that what makes divisibility by 3 objective is the fact that any dispute about it can be settled by appeal to a certain *procedure*. For example, if Jones claims that 22 is divisible by 3, he can be proved wrong by showing him the multiplication table and pointing out that 22 is not in the "3" column (i.e., is not a multiple of 3).[4] On the other hand, no procedure has been stated for un-

---

[4] Similarly, in the case of putting pegs into holes, a certain procedure is involved, namely, picking up a peg, placing the end of it in line with the

thinkability which could be used to settle disputes about it. All that was said was "try to think it". But this cannot settle any disputes. It does not provide any procedure to which we could appeal in order to prove an opponent wrong. If a person says that he is or is not able to think a given proposition, then we cannot prove him wrong, for we have nothing objective to appeal to as we do in the case of divisibility by 3. Therefore, unthinkability is a purely subjective property. We can apply it to propositions only on the basis of how we personally feel about them, and any serious non-verbal dispute about whether or not a given proposition is unthinkable is immediately insoluble. This proves that P is true after all. What is unthinkable for one person may not be unthinkable for another. Thus, since unthinkability is a subjective property, it cannot be used as the basis for any adequate theory of type crossings.

I believe that this is the most important objection to the analogy between unthinkability and divisibility by 3,[5] and also the most important defense of principle P. I have two replies to it, the first of which may be called "the argument from presupposed agreement".

It was claimed that any dispute about divisibility by 3 can be settled by appeal to a certain procedure. If Jones claims that 22 is divisible by 3, he can be proved wrong by showing him the multiplication table and pointing out that 22 is not in the "3" column. But to say that this would settle the dispute, at least in

---

hole, and then applying pressure to the peg in the direction of the hole. According to the objection, it is the possibility of appealing to a procedure such as this that makes "fittability" an objective property.

[5] Another objection is that the question of whether or not a number is divisible by 3 could be decided by means of a machine, and it is this which makes the property objective. But I am sure that a machine could also be programmed in such a way as to distinguish thinkable propositions from unthinkable propositions. A list of types would have to be worked out for this purpose (among other things), and it might be quite difficult in actual practice, but I see no theoretical difficulty preventing it. Therefore, this objection does not succeed in weakening the analogy between thinkability and divisibility by 3.

one sense of 'settle',[6] *presupposes* that Jones will agree that 22 is not in the "3" column. Suppose Jones does not acknowledge that. Suppose Jones, looking at the multiplication table, claims that 22 *is* in the "3" column. What then? How is the dispute to be settled? Perhaps a straight edge could be produced, and one end placed at the top of the column and the other end at the bottom: then the fact that the numeral '22' is not contiguous with a part of the straight edge would establish that the number 22 is not in that column. But Jones may claim that the numeral '22' *is* contiguous with a part of the straight edge, or he may claim that the edge is not straight but quite curved. What can be said then? It seems that eventually a sort of disagreement will be reached which cannot be settled by appeal to any procedure. It is clear that any appeal to a procedure to settle a dispute will always depend upon a certain agreement between the disputants as regards the way the procedure is to be used, its application to the case in question, and so on. And if there is no such agreement about these matters, then the dispute will simply not be settled. To put it another way, since there are always points of application over which disagreement could arise, no procedure can, by its very nature, guarantee that the disputes to which it is applied will be settled. To say that the appeal to a given procedure will settle

---

[6] The sense of 'settle' to which I am appealing here is that in which a dispute is settled if and only if the opponents come to agree with one another about the matter at issue. In another sense of 'settle', a dispute is settled if and only if the truth about the matter has been stated in such a clear way that any further disagreement would be irrational. But this second sense of 'settle' is of no use in the discussion, for disputes about unthinkability *can* be settled in accordance with it, just as disputes about divisibility by 3 can. For example, if I say that the proposition that the theory of relativity is blue is unthinkable and Jones says that it is not unthinkable, then the dispute has already been settled in the sense in question; for, in my statement that the proposition is unthinkable, the truth about the matter *was* stated in such a clear way that any further disagreement would be irrational. Anyone who says of an unthinkable proposition, such as the proposition that the theory of relativity is blue, that it is not unthinkable is being quite irrational. Thus, since the second sense of 'settle' does not serve to draw any distinction between thinkability and divisibility by 3, I shall appeal only to the first sense in my discussion of the objection.

a certain kind of dispute invariably presupposes that there will be agreement about the application of the procedure in individual cases. But such agreement cannot be guaranteed. Hence, any dispute may turn out to be ultimately insoluble, even disputes about whether or not a given number is divisible by 3. Thus, we must conclude that a predicate may be objective even though insoluble disputes can arise with respect to its application.

It may be objected that I am here appealing to absurd cases, that to speak of a person who claims that 22 is in the "3" column of the multiplication table is to speak of something far-fetched and ridiculous. But that is just my point. Of course it is far-fetched and ridiculous, but so would be the example of a person claiming that the theory of relativity can be thought of as being blue. The analogy here is quite close. So, if there is justification in assuming that no disagreement will ever arise over the application of certain procedures, then I should think one is justified in assuming that no disagreement will ever arise over the thinkability or unthinkability of propositions. As a matter of fact, I do not know of any place in the whole literature of philosophy or any other field where such disagreement has ever taken place. Philosophers may disagree radically about the application of many other predicates, but with regard to the application of the term 'unthinkable' to propositions, their opinion, at least as far as I know, has been quite uniform.

It has been maintained that propositions now known to be empirically false were at one time held to be *self-evident* (i.e., having an unthinkable negation). But I have yet to see any convincing illustration of this. The example of the Earth being flat will not do, because no one ever held that to be self-evident in any relevant sense. The example of physical space being Euclidean will not do, because that proposition is not now known to be empirically false. It seems unlikely to me that any example will be found that would do. Unlike the concept of a subject matter, the concept of thinkability is not time-dependent. What is thinkable today was thinkable 5000 years ago. What was self-evident 5000 years ago is self-evident today. The main reason why we think propositions today that people did not think at that time is that we have the basic material for such propositions, namely, the individual concepts that go to make them up. If people 5000 years ago had had the individual concepts that we have today, then they would have been able to combine them in thought just as we do today.

Consider, now, an appeal to a different sort of procedure in the case of divisibility by 3. Suppose it is argued that the way to prove Jones wrong when he claims that 22 is divisible by 3, and thereby prove the objectivity of divisibility by 3, is to define the concepts "22" and "divisible by 3" in terms of purely logical concepts and then to deduce the proposition that 22 is not divisible by 3 from the axioms of arithmetic (also expressed in terms of purely logical concepts). But does this necessarily settle the dispute? Not at all. Jones may do any number of odd things: he may deny the truth of the axioms of arithmetic or he may deny the truth of the principles of logic which are appealed to in the proof. And, in such a case, the dispute would be insoluble, for no procedure could be brought forward to establish that the axioms of arithmetic are true or that the principles of logic are true. Therefore, even where logical proof is appealed to, the statement that the procedure will settle any given dispute presupposes that the disputants will agree on certain basic questions underlying the procedure. Thus, although an appeal to the thinkability test [7] presupposes that no disagreement will arise about its application to particular cases, this is true of any test or procedure. In particular, it is true for any procedure that defines divisibility by 3. In this respect, thinkability and divisibility by 3 are quite analogous.

The only essential difference between thinkability and divisi-

[7] The test may be stated as follows: "try to think the proposition; if you succeed, then it is thinkable; if not, then it is unthinkable". I see no objection to calling this a "procedure", except that it would have to be just a "one-step procedure". If it is insisted that a test must consist in at least two or three steps in order to be regarded a *procedure,* then I shall go along and say of the thinkability test that it is only a test and not a procedure. Nothing much turns on this, however.

bility by 3 is that disputes about the latter concept are a little further removed from insoluble disagreement than disputes about the former concept. But this is not a difference that has anything to do with subjectivity and objectivity. It only reflects the fact that thinkability is not a logically complex concept, as is divisibility by 3, for it is defined only in terms of a one-step test, whereas the latter concept is defined in terms of a multi-step test (or procedure).

This concludes "the argument from presupposed agreement", which constitutes my first reply to the objection to the analogy between thinkability and divisibility by 3. I have, however, another reply. It may still be claimed that it is the fact that divisibility by 3 is logically complex that makes that concept objective. My reply to this is that being logically complex is not a necessary condition for being being objective. There are properties which are objective but which are not logically complex. As an example, consider the property of redness.

Redness is an objective property because it would be absurd to suggest that what is red for one person may not be red for another. It is important to distinguish here between the property of redness, or *being* red, and the property of *looking* red. Whereas looking red is a subjective property (in that it makes perfectly good sense to say that a given object looks red to one person but not to another), *being* red is objective rather than subjective. Yet redness is not a logically complex property. The test for whether or not an object is red is simply to look at it and see what color it is. There is no multi-step procedure involved here.[8] The case of redness is analogous to the case of unthinkability, where the test for whether or not a proposition is unthinkable is simply to try to think it.

Suppose we have an object before us which is clearly red (say,

[8]   It may be claimed that the test for redness involves spectroscopic analysis of the light emitted from the object. But this is a mistake. Children know nothing about spectroscopes, yet they do know what 'red' means; nor has that word changed in meaning since the correlation between color and wave length was discovered. Furthermore, there are things which are red but which do not emit light at all, as, for example, after-images.

fresh blood). And suppose Jones comes along and claims that the object is not red. We would say that there are just two possibilities: either he is using the word 'red' differently from us (which includes the case of color-blindness) or else he is simply not to be taken seriously. But on what grounds do we say this? It is on the grounds of our general agreement that the object in question is red and that if anyone denies this, then he must somehow be wrong. In other words, there is general agreement that redness is a property *of the object* and does not depend upon the state of the viewer or on his relationship to the object.

As a contrast, consider two properties, in addition to the property of *looking* red, which are clearly subjective. I have in mind the properties of being familiar and tasting too sweet. Suppose there is a piece of music which most people would say is familiar, e.g., the British national anthem. And suppose Jones, after listening to this music, claims that it is not familiar. In this case, we would not say that Jones is wrong or mistaken; we would simply acknowledge that the music is unfamiliar *to him*. Similarly, suppose Jones were to drink an ordinary-sized cocktail containing five teaspoons of sugar, which most people would say tastes too sweet. And suppose Jones claims that the drink does not taste too sweet. Again, we would not say that Jones is wrong or mistaken; we would simply acknowledge that his taste in drinks is different from that of most people.

In both of these cases, the property is interpreted as inhering in the person who does the listening or tasting (or in his relationship to the object) rather than in the object itself. And this fact is reflected in the way we react to such situations as those described above. Whereas it cannot be allowed that what is generally agreed to be red may not be red for Jones, it *can* certainly be allowed that what is generally agreed to be familiar (or to taste too sweet) may not be familiar (or may not taste too sweet) to Jones. The criterion for objectivity of a property, then, is not the possibility of appealing to some sort of procedure, but rather, is the reaction of people to a departure from what is generally agreed to be the set of things to which the property applies. If the person making such a departure is not regarded as wrong or mistaken (but rather, right "from his own perspective"), then the property is subjective; otherwise it is objective. This difference between subjectivity and objectivity of properties may be thought of as a difference in what is sometimes called the "logical grammars" of the predicates which designate them.

By means of this analogy with redness, I hope to have shown that a property can be objective even though it is logically simple. Hence, the fact that unthinkability is logically simple does not constitute a reason for denying that it is objective or for believing principle P. I conclude from this, together with what was said above, that there is no disanalogy between unthinkability and divisibility by 3 which could constitute a reason for saying that the latter concept is objective, but not the former. My view is that the two properties are perfectly analogous in this respect, and I hope to have adequately answered the objection to my view which made appeal to the concept of a *procedure*.

So far, my reasoning has been largely negative, attacking all arguments in support of principle P. Now I propose to be more positive, by applying the criterion of objectivity, which was introduced above, directly to unthinkability. Suppose Jones were to claim that the proposition that the theory of relativity is blue is not unthinkable, because *he* is able to think it. What would we say to this? Would we say that he is somehow wrong (i.e., that he is using his words differently from us or else is not being serious) or would we allow that *he* really can think the proposition in question, even thought we cannot? It is clear, I think, that we must take the former alternative. The latter alternative involves an absurdity, for if Jones can think the proposition that the theory of relativity is blue, then it must be (conceptually) possible for the theory of relativity to be blue. But we cannot allow the possibility of blue theories any more than we can allow the possibility of square circles or the possibility of 22 being divisible by 3. It follows that unthinkability must be an objective property. In other words, whether or not a proposition is unthinkable depends on what the proposition is, not on who is attempting to think it. Principle P, then, must me false.

To press the matter further, let us consider in greater detail the various alternatives open to us if Jones were to claim that *he* is able to think the proposition that the theory of relativity is blue. The first alternative is that when Jones talks about what he calls "the proposition that the theory of relativity is blue", he is not talking about the same proposition that I have been talking about when I used the words "the proposition that the theory of relativity is blue". For example, Jones might be taking the expression 'theory of relativity' to refer to some physical object (such as a book) rather than to an abstract entity. Or perhaps he is using the predicate 'is blue' in some metaphorical sense. In either case, Jones's claim would not give us any reason to believe that the proposition which is unthinkable for us (namely, a certain abstract entity having a certain color) is not unthinkable for Jones as well, for he would not even be talking about *that* proposition. It is clear that, in order to establish the subjectivity of unthinkability, a case must be produced where *one and the same* proposition is unthinkable for one person and not for another.

A second alternative open to us is to deny that Jones is using the term 'think' in our sense. When he claims that he can think the proposition that the theory of relativity is blue, he may not mean that he can qualitatively imagine what it would be like for that proposition to be true. He may mean merely that he is familiar with the logical form of the proposition (or something to that effect). In such a case, Jones's claim that he can think the proposition may very well be true in his sense of 'think'. But it need not be true in our sense of 'think'. This same point is perhaps more crucial in a case where Jones claims a proposition to be unthinkable which we would say is not unthinkable. Suppose, for example, Jones were to claim that it is unthinkable for water to boil at room temperature at normal pressure. What I would suggest here is that Jones is not using the term 'unthinkable' in our sense, but rather, means by it something like "empirically impossible". This would be confirmed if he were to justify his classification of the proposition in question on the grounds that it would violate the physical laws governing the boiling point of water. In such a case, Jones's claim that the proposition is unthinkable would be true in his sense of 'unthinkable'. But it would not follow that the proposition is unthinkable, even for Jones, in our sense of 'unthinkable'. In order to establish that a proposition is unthinkable for someone in our sense of 'unthinkable', more is needed than just the person's claim that it is unthinkable for him. It must at least be ascertained that the person is using the term 'unthinkable' in our sense.

The position I am defending is that if Jones claims that a proposition which we say is unthinkable is not unthinkable (or that a proposition which we say is not unthinkable is unthinkable) and the two alternatives, described above, are ruled out, then we must conclude that Jones is not to be taken seriously. Now, it might be suggested that there should be a fourth alternative – one which would correspond to the possibility of *miscalculation* in the case of divisibility by 3. In other words, just as we might conclude that Jones made a mistake in calculation if he were to say that 32532 is not divisible by 3, so also we should be able to say that he made a *mistake in thinking* if he were to claim to be able to think the proposition that the theory of relativity is blue. The reason I do not consider this a possibility is that there does not seem to be any way to distinguish it from the first two alternatives, which involve the disputant's use of words. Determining unthinkability is not like determining divisibility by 3 in that it could require calculation. And this is true of complex propositions as well as simple ones.

To bring this out by means of an example, let us consider a complex sentence which is logically equivalent to "the theory of relativity is blue", such as the following:

T: The proposition which results from ascribing the property which is ascribed to the sky over Ithaca in the proposition that the sky over Ithaca is blue to the entity denoted by the direct object of the sentence "Einstein formulated the theory of relativity" is true.

If Jones were to claim that the proposition expressed by T is thinkable whereas the proposition that the theory of relativity is blue is unthinkable, it would simply be a case where he does not realize that they are one and the same proposition.[9] In a certain sense of 'understand', which I shall call linguistic understanding", he would be failing to understand T. A person linguistically understands a sentence if and only if he knows the relevant meaning of each word in the sentence and also all the logical relations of the sentence with other sentences. In other words, all that is required for linguistic understanding of a sentence is knowledge of its vocabulary and syntax. Thus, it is possible to linguistically understand a type crossing. All this comes to is knowing *what* proposition the type crossing expresses; it does not require being able to think that proposition.[10] In the case of T, if Jones does not see that it is logically equivalent to "the theory of relativity is blue", then he would be failing to linguistically understand the sentence. Rather than saying that Jones made a mistake in thinking the proposition expressed by T, it would be more accurate to say that he does not know (or is not aware of) what that proposition is. A person might very well make a mistake in deciding what proposition a given sentence expresses. And this would be brought out by his incorrect answers to

[9] I do not mean to imply that *any* two logically equivalent sentences must express the same proposition. That this is not so may be seen from the fact that every logically true sentence is logically equivalent to every other. However, for certain types of sentences, the criterion for whether or not they express the same proposition is that of whether or not they are logically equivalent. And sentence T together with "the theory of relativity is blue" are, I believe, of this sort.

[10] With regard to the model of putting pegs into holes, the analogy to a sentence being linguistically meaningful would be simply someone trying to put a peg into a hole. However, the analogy to a sentence expressing a thinkable proposition would be the peg *fitting into* the hole. One can know what peg and what hole a person is working with without necessarily being able to fit the peg into the hole. Similarly, one can know what proposition a given sentence is supposed to express without necessarily being able to think the proposition. And just as we cannot determine whether a peg fits into a hole unless we know what the peg and hole are (e.g., by seeing or touching them), so also we cannot determine whether the proposition expressed by a given sentence is thinkable unless we know what the proposition is (i.e., unless we linguistically understand the given sentence).

questions about the logical relationships of the sentence to other sentences. However, such a situation is certainly not to be described as a case of making a mistake in thinking a given proposition. Indeed, it is not clear what a mistake of that sort could possibly be like.[11]

The analogy in the case of divisibility by 3 would be that in which a person with normal powers of calculation tries to divide a number by 3, claims to succeed (using his terms in the same sense as we do), and checks and rechecks his result, but the number is really indivisible by 3. It just is not clear how this is possible or what sort of "mistake" might be involved. The analogy in the case of redness would be that in which a person with normal vision, using the term 'red' in the same sense as we do, says of an object that it is red, when in reality it is a quite different color, say, green. And the analogy in the case of a peg fitting into a hole would be that in which a psychologically normal person, using his terms in the same sense as we do, claims to have put a peg into a hole, when in reality the peg does not fit into the hole. What sort of mistake could he have made? Just as it is not clear what sorts of mistakes are involved here, so also it is not clear how a person who knows what proposition a given sentence expresses could make a mistake about whether it is thinkable or unthinkable. These are the sorts of mistakes the possibility of which I must deny.

Perhaps a still clearer way to show the various analogies is in terms of the following four definitions:

(1) 'Number n is divisible by 3' means 'any person with normal powers of calculation is able to divide n (evenly) by 3'.
(2) 'Object O is red' means 'O would look red to any normal person who observes O under normal conditions'.
(3) 'Peg P fits into hole H' means 'any physically normal person is able to put P into H'.

---

[11] This is closely related to the conclusion reached in Chapter 4, where is was argued (on pages 64-66) that there are no such things as "category mistakes" if they are understood to be something more than mere mistakes in vocabulary.

(4) 'Proposition p is thinkable' means 'any person who knows what p is (i.e., who linguistically understands at least one sentence which expresses p) is able to think p'.

The fact that a person with subnormal powers of calculation is unable to divide a given number (evenly) by 3 is irrelevant to the question whether or not that number is divisible by 3. Similarly, the fact that a given object does not look red to a color blind person or to a person in a dark room is irrelevant to the question whether or not the object is red. Also, the fact that a paralyzed person is unable to put a given peg into a given hole is irrelevant to the question whether or not the peg fits into the hole. In a similar way, the fact that a person who does not know what a given proposition is is unable to think that proposition is irrelevant to the question whether or not that proposition is thinkable. Sometimes it takes a great amount of study to linguistically understand a given sentence and thereby know what proposition it expresses. Any highly technical sentence or a sentence from a difficult foreign language would serve as an example of this point. The layman is unable to think the propositions expressed by such sentences because he simply does not know what those propositions are. But it does not in any way follow that the propositions are unthinkable. They may or may not be thinkable. This will depend on whether or not people who do know what the propositions are (i.e., who linguistically understand sentences expressing them) are able to think them.

There is a distinction to be drawn between "Jones is able to divide n by 3" and "n is divisible by 3 for Jones". Whereas the former is a meaningful statement about Jones's abilities at calculating, the latter is a meaningless remark which presupposes that divisibility by 3 is a subjective concept. Similar distinctions are to be drawn between "O looks red to Jones" and "O is red to Jones", and between "Jones is able to put peg P into hole H" and "peg P fits into hole H for Jones". In each case, the former remark is intelligible, but not the latter. In a similar way, a distinction is to be drawn between "Jones is able to think p" and "p is thinkable for Jones". The former statement is meaningful, its truth or falsity depending on two issues: whether or not Jones knows what p is and whether or not p is thinkable. But the latter statement is quite unintelligible. Similarly, principle P, that what is unthinkable for one person may not be unthinkable for another, is also unintelligible. It makes no more sense than would the corresponding subjectivist principles in the cases of divisibility by 3, redness, and "fittability". To put it another way, if anyone who linguistically understands a given sentence is unable to think the proposition which it expresses, then that proposition must be unthinkable *for everyone* in the same sense in which a number which is indivisible by 3 is indivisible by 3 for everyone, and in which a red object is red for everyone, and in which a peg which fits into a hole fits into it for everyone. The expression 'for everyone' here indicates that the property is objective and that the subjectivist's principle cannot be meaningfully applied to it.

Suppose someone, say Jones, were to claim to be able to think a proposition which we say is unthinkable, and it is ascertained both that he is referring to the same proposition as we do and that he is using the term 'think' in our sense. In that case, we *must* simply refuse to take Jones seriously, for there are only two other alternatives, namely, to allow that he really *can* think the proposition in question or else to take him to have made some sort of mistake in thinking (a "category mistake"), and both of these have been shown to be absurd. First of all, it is just as senseless to speak of Jones as being able to think a proposition which we know to be unthinkable as it is to speak of him as being able to (evenly) divide a number by 3 which we know to be indivisible by 3. And secondly, it is just as senseless to speak of Jones as making a mistake in thinking (under the given conditions) as it is to speak of him as making a mistake in dividing by 3 under the conditions where he has ordinary powers of calculation, is using all relevant terms in the same sense as we do, checks and rechecks his result an indefinite number of times, and yet comes to a different conclusion than we do with respect to a given number. Similar analogies can be drawn in the case of our other two objective properties: redness and "fittability". The fact that, under the given conditions, we must refuse to take Jones seriously, and cannot allow that he really *is* able to think the proposition in question, entails that unthinkability is an objective concept. It is a concept which is in the same category with divisibility by 3, redness, and "fittability" (and *not* in the same category with familiarity, tasting too sweet, and looking red). And, finally, all philosophical and critical questions about it can be answered by appeal to those three analogies.

What I mean by this last remark is that the three analogies provide a strong basis for defending the concept of unthinkability against the many objections and critical questions that philosophers are inclined to put to it. For example, a philosopher may want to ask: "Is being unable to think a given proposition a substantial limitation, like being unable to lift 500 pounds?" The reply: "It is the same sort of limitation as being unable to divide 22 by 3, whatever sort that may be." Here are some other objections and their corresponding replies:

Objection	Reply
1. How do you know when you have succeeded in thinking a proposition?	1. It is the same way you know you have succeeded in putting a peg into a hole – you simply observe the result (except in the case of thinking a proposition, you observe the result in your "mind's eye").
2. Inasmuch as lower animals are unable to think certain propositions that humans *are* able to think, it must be that thinkability does depend on who is doing the thinking, after all.	2. This argument is just as foolish as claiming that inasmuch as lower animals are unable to divide certain numbers by 3 which humans *are* able to divide by 3, it must be that divisibility by 3 depends on who is doing the dividing.
3. If someone disagrees with you about the thinkability of	3. It is the same justification you have in assuming that if

a given proposition, you immediately *assume* that he is either using his terms differently or else is not to be taken seriously. But what justification is there in assuming that?

someone disagrees with you about the divisibility by 3 of a given number, then either you or he has made a mistake in calculating or is using words differently or else is not to be taken seriously. No other alternative is intelligible.

4. How can you teach the concept of thinkability to someone who does not know what it is?

4. You teach it the same way as in the case of, say, redness. That is, you point out positive and negative instances, and give as good a verbal definition as is possible. Apply the technique used in Section 7.2.

5. What do you do with someone who still does not understand the concept of thinkability, despite all that has been said?

5. You do the same as with someone who is unable to understand the concept of redness despite all your explanations. You either give up or else keep on trying.

This list of objections is not exhaustive, but it does serve to illustrate how the three analogies can be of use in defense of the concept of unthinkability. In my opinion, such a defense can be given against all possible objections, but whether or not I am right can only be settled through further investigation and dialectic.[12]

---

[12]   The question may arise as to how we are to interpret the results of the present section in terms of the five points which were listed at the end of section 7.2 as a partial explanation of the concept of unthinkability. There are two ways to interpret it. If unthinkability is defined just in terms of points 1-4, then the present section may be construed as an argument to the effect that unthinkability is an objective concept. On the other hand, if point 5, which *states* that unthinkability is objective, is included in the definition, then the present section may be construed as an argument that unthinkability is a self-consistent concept, or, in other words, that point 5 is perfectly consistent with points 1-4.

7.4. BORDERLINE CASES

It was said that redness is an objective property. But there are objects which represent borderline cases of red, for example, objects which have a color between red and orange which some people might call red and others might call orange. In these cases there is no general agreement as to whether the object is red or not red. Is redness really objective then? I would say that it is objective, but there is no general agreement on any exact boundary for it. In other words, a property could be objective but still *vague*.

This brings us to the third main objection to unthinkability – that, like redness, it is a vague concept, and therefore, if it is used as the basis of one's theory of type crossings, it would make the concept of a type crossing vague as well. There would then be sentences of which we could not say that they are type crossings or that they are not type crossings. They would be borderline cases.

We can put the issue this way: although there are propositions which are clearly thinkable (e.g., the proposition that water boils at room temperature) and propositions which are clearly unthinkable (e.g., the proposition that the theory of relativity is blue), it may be that not all propositions are so clear-cut. Consider, for example, the graded series of propositions which was given as an illustration in Chapter 1 and which reads as follows:

(a) Englishmen like coffee better than tea.
(b) Squirrels like coffee better than tea.
(c) Protozoa like coffee better than tea.
(d) Bacteria like coffee better than tea.
(e) Milkweed plants like coffee better than tea.
(f) Stones like coffee better than tea.
(g) Electrons like coffee better than tea.
(h) Quadratic equations like coffee better than tea.

We can see that (a) is clearly thinkable and (h) is clearly unthinkable. But what of the other propositions? Must we come to the conclusion that the difference between the thinkable and the unthinkable, like the difference between red and orange, is not sharp, but only one of degree?

It is my position that the difference is not one of degree. A line can be drawn across the above list of propositions to distinguish the thinkable from the unthinkable. To see where this line should go, let us consider the example in detail. First of all, what is the ordinary criterion for something, say x, liking drink A better than drink B? Roughly, it is that whenever x is to make a free choice between A and B (i.e., a choice in which there is no external force influencing it), x invariably chooses A rather than B. We can conclude, then, that if x is capable of making a free choice between two drinks or foodstuffs, then it is thinkable for x to like one of them better than the other. So, the question to ask is which of the subjects of propositions (a)–(h) is capable of making a free choice between coffee and tea.

It is clear, I think, that the subjects of (a) and (b) are capable of such, but that the subjects of (g) and (h) are not. Therefore, (a) and (b) are thinkable, whereas (g) and (h) are unthinkable. Now what about the subjects of (c) and (d): protozoa and bacteria? There is not much difficulty about protozoa, because they are all capable of both ingestion and movement. If, under the microscope, it were observed that protozoa, when given the opportunity, tend to ingest particles of coffee, but avoid particles of tea, then the phenomenon might quite properly be described as in (c). Therefore, (c) is thinkable. What about (d), then? (d) presents a certain problem in that bacteria, so far as I know, are not capable of ingesting particles of matter. On the other hand, if things which resemble bacteria in all other respects were to be observed ingesting particles of coffee, I believe they would still be called "bacteria". Furthermore, if normal bacteria tend to move towards particles of coffee and away from particles of tea, then I do not think there would be any stretching of ordinary usage in describing the phenomenon as in (d). So, for both of these reasons, I would classify (d) as thinkable.

Consider now proposition (f). Suppose something which has the chemical composition of a stone were to be capable of self-movement and thus choice. Would we call it a stone? In this case, I think the answer is No. Here the departure is too radical. If we were convinced that the object is moving itself, rather than being moved by something else, then we could not call it a "stone" no matter what its chemical composition is found to be. Therefore, (f) must be regarded as an unthinkable proposition.

It is proposition (e) which has the greatest likelihood of being a "borderline case". Suppose scientists were to discover a kind of thing which looks and is constructed exactly like a milkweed plant, but is capable of locomotion. It can pull up its roots and crawl from one place to another, and then "replant" itself there. The question is: would we consider such a thing a new species of milkweed plant or something else entirely? I believe that, as in the case of the stone, the thing could not be called a milkweed plant. Must we conclude, then, that (e) is unthinkable?

Consider this possibility, which was suggested to me by Dr. Charles Parsons. A milkweed plant is planted on a border on one side of which the soil is impregnated with coffee and on the other side of which the soil is impregnated with tea; in all other respects the two sides are identical. Then suppose the plant grows more roots on the coffee side. Would we say that it likes coffee better than tea? This problem is complicated by the fact that there is a somewhat metaphorical use of the verb 'to like' in which a farmer might say of his crop that it "likes" fertilizer A better than fertilizer B, meaning that it *thrives* better on A than on B.

In this sense of liking, milkweed plants might of course be said to like coffee better than tea (if they thrived better on coffee, used as fertilizer, than on tea). But this metaphorical use of the verb is quite distinct from the literal use in which 'liking' is to be defined in terms of 'choosing'. Clearly, the milkweed plant in our hypothetical case cannot be said to "choose" the coffee-impregnated soil. Rather, it seems to be more a case of its *thriving* better in that soil. Therefore, we can say that the

milkweed plant "likes" coffee better than tea only in the metaphorical sense of 'like' mentioned above. If we stick to the literal
use of the verb, then proposition (e) should be classified as unthinkable. It would be thinkable, however, if 'like' is interpreted
in the metaphorical sense.[13] At any rate, once it is decided what
'like' is to mean in propositions (a)–(h), there is no longer any
vagueness about where the line is to go to separate the thinkable
propositions from the unthinkable propositions. If 'like' is understood in the literal sense, then the line is to go between (d) and
(e); if it is understood in the metaphorical sense, then obviously
it is to go between (e) and (f). There is no element of degree
involved at all.

The way to decide whether or not a proposition is thinkable
is to analyze the concepts it contains. Sometimes it is not immediately clear how a given concept is to be analyzed or interpreted. For example, the question "could x like A better than B
if x could not be said to *choose* A rather than B?" is crucial to the
issue of whether or not proposition (e) is thinkable. If one person
were to answer the question "yes" and another were to answer it
"no", then there would be *two* concepts of liking involved, and
hence *two* propositions which could be expressed in the same
words as (e). One of the propositions would be thinkable, the
other not. There would be no element of degree at all. In some
cases, it is difficult to decide whether or not a given sentence
expresses a thinkable proposition, but this is never due to any
vagueness in the notion of thinkability. Rather, it is due to the
difficulty of deciding what proposition the sentence expresses.
This is often difficult because of what is called the "open texture" of one or more of the words in the sentence. Once this open
texture is resolved by giving the words a more precise meaning,
the question of thinkability is settled automatically.

To illustrate this point further, I shall list several sentences

---

[13]   In the bacteria case, the literal use of the verb 'to like' is much more
applicable, for it would be quite in order to ask: "which side (of the visual
field of the microscope) did the bacteria *choose,* the left side or the right
side?"

about which it may be difficult to decide whether they express thinkable propositions or unthinkable propositions. They are as follows:

(81) The seat of the bed is hard.
(82) A lion's trunk is shorter than an elephant's trunk.
(83) That baby is embarrassed.
(84) The United States is blue.
(85) Bacteria drink dust.

In each case, the question of whether or not the sentence expresses an unthinkable proposition is a question about how certain concepts are to be analyzed or interpreted. The following remarks show how this is so:

Sentence (81) expresses a thinkable proposition only if an object which looks like a bed, but has a seat or bench attached to it, would normally be called a bed.

Sentence (82) expresses a thinkable proposition only if an animal which looks like a lion, except that it has a trunk, would normally be called a lion (or a new species of lion).

Sentence (83) expresses a thinkable proposition only if a baby (say, someone under age one) who presents all of the behavioral manifestations of being embarrassed (including whatever adult talk would be part of such manifestations) would normally be said to be embarrassed.

Sentence (84) expresses a thinkable proposition only if there is some aspect of the physical territory of the United States (possibly its soil, for example) such that, if all of it turned blue, then the United States might normally be described as turning or being blue.

Sentence (85) expresses a thinkable proposition only if the ingestion of dust particles by what appear (from their cell structure) to be bacteria would normally be described as *bacteria drinking dust*.

It is understood, of course, that the sentences are to be interpreted literally rather than metaphorically.[14] In many cases it may be difficult to analyze the relevant concepts in terms of the question suggested in the remark. But it is only when the concepts are thus analyzed that the issue of thinkability and unthinkability can be settled.

Another way to put this is to say that whenever there is difficulty in deciding of a sentence whether or not it expresses an unthinkable proposition, it is invariably a difficulty in pinpointing the linguistic meaning of the sentence. The question is never "is *this* proposition thinkable or not?" Rather, it is "what proposition is this sentence supposed to express?" And this question can be answered only by analyzing or interpreting the meaning of the words in the sentence. Once it is decided what proposition a sentence expresses, there is no longer any problem about whether or not it is a thinkable proposition. For, as was argued at length in Section 7.3, it would be absurd to suggest that a person could know what proposition a sentence expresses and yet not know whether or not he is able to think that proposition. Therefore, there are no borderline cases as far as the thinkability or unthinkability of propositions is concerned. Unthinkability differs from redness in that it is in no way a vague concept; it does not admit of degree. In this respect it is again analogous to divisibility by 3.

After all that has been said, I shall assume that the concept of unthinkability is now sufficiently clear for me to use it in the clarification of other concepts, for that is what I shall do in the next section. I hope to have at least shown that the concept of unthinkability contains dialectical resources on the basis of which it can be defended against the main objections to it.

---

[14] I do not mean to suggest that the line separating the metaphorical uses of a term from its literal uses is always sharp and clear. In many instances, what was once a metaphorical use has become almost literal (e.g., "she planted an idea in his mind"). However, I do not believe that this is the case with any of the terms in sentences (79)–(83). So they need not cause any difficulty in that respect.

7.5. NECESSITY AND MEANINGLESSNESS

It was pointed out that unthinkability shares with redness a feature not possessed by divisibility by 3, namely, the fact that they are logically simple properties. However, there are *many* features shared by unthinkability and divisibility by 3 which are not possessed by redness; among these are the fact that they apply to abstract entities (propositions and numbers, respectively), the fact that there is no vagueness about them with respect to their application to those entities, and the fact that they are *essential* properties. Let us briefly consider this last point.

An object can be the thing it is (a pencil, blood, the sky, etc.) whether it is red or not red; and it can change from red to not red (or vice versa) and still be the thing it is. Thus, redness is not an essential property of objects. On the other hand, if a number is divisible by 3, then it cannot change to being not divisible by 3 (or vice versa) and still be the same number. Divisibility by 3 is an essential property of numbers. Similarly, unthinkability is an essential property. If a proposition is unthinkable, then it cannot become thinkable (or vice versa) and still be the same proposition. Another way to express this distinction is to say that whereas sentences of the form "x is red" are always *contingent* truths or falsehoods, sentences of the form 'n is divisible by 3" and "p is unthinkable" are always *necessary* truths or falsehoods.[15]

But now a question arises. What makes sentences of the form "p is unthinkable" necessary? It can be plausibly argued that sentences of the form "n is divisible by 3" are necessary because they can be proved true or false on the basis of the reducibility of arithmetic to logic. In other words, all sentences of the form

---

[15] Here, 'n' and 'p' are to be understood as representing *names* (of specific numbers and propositions, respectively) rather than descriptive phrases (or phrases which leave doubt as to what is being referred to). Thus, "21 is divisible by 3" is of the form "n is divisible by 3", but not "the number of peanuts in this bag is divisible by 3". Also, "that the theory of relativity drinks whiskey is unthinkable" is of the form "p is unthinkable", but not "the proposition expressed by Jones's third utterance is unthinkable".

"n is divisible by 3" can be thought of as complex definitional truths or falsehoods. But this is not so in the case of "p is unthinkable". What, then, is the basis of the necessity of "p is unthinkable"? Why must all sentences of the form "p is unthinkable" be either necessarily true or necessarily false?

The reason is that if a proposition is unthinkable, then it is unthinkable that anyone should be able to think it (i.e., that it be thinkable).[16] And if a proposition is thinkable, then it is unthinkable that anyone who knows what it is should be unable to think it (i.e., that it be unthinkable). But every proposition is either thinkable or unthinkable (in the exclusive sense). Therefore, the following statement is true:

A: For every proposition, p, either it is unthinkable for p to be unthinkable or it is unthinkable for p to be not unthinkable.

So, by virtue of the following definition:

Definition B: "p is necessarily true" means "it is unthinkable, for p to be false" (or "not-p is unthinkable"),

it follows logically from statement A that all sentences of the form "p is unthinkable" are either necessarily true or necessarily false.

But what is the justification for Definition B? In this regard, it must be remembered that unthinkability is the same as conceptual impossibility. By virtue of the rule that a proposition is necessary if and only if its negation is impossible, it follows that a proposition is conceptually necessary if and only if its negation is unthinkable. But being conceptually necessary is the same as being necessary. So, as it turns out, all the following propositional forms are equivalent:

p is necessary

p is necessarily true

---

[16]   Although "that the theory of relativity is blue is thinkable" expresses an unthinkable proposition, it is not a type crossing, for its subject designates a proposition, which is certainly the *type* of thing which can be thinkable. On the other hand, a sentence such as "Socrates is thinkable" not only expresses an unthinkable proposition, but is a type crossing as well.

p is conceptually necessary
p is true a priori
not-p is impossible
not-p is necessarily false
not-p is conceptually impossible
not-p is false a priori
not-p is unthinkable.

There are two objections to Definition B which I would like to consider. The first objection is that, on the basis of Definition B, it is always open to any metaphysician to claim that his statements about the ultimate nature of reality are necessary truths on the grounds that he is unable to think the propositions expressed by their negations and therefore those negations must be necessarily false. Furthermore, there could be no basis for rejecting what he says.

My reply to this objection is that the question of whether or not a sequence expresses an unthinkable proposition can be answered only by appeal to those who know what the proposition is (if there is any) that the sequence is supposed to express. Until a person knows what proposition a metaphysician's statement is supposed to express, he cannot say either that it is an unthinkable proposition or that it is a thinkable proposition. And this applies also to the negation of the metaphysician's statement.

To take an example, consider a sentence selected at random from Jean-Paul Sartre's *Being and Nothingness:*

S: The nothingness of being, which is priority in relation to an "appeared" which "was not", can some only retrospectively to a world by a For-itself which is its own nothingness and its own priority.[17]

Sentence S is linguistically meaningless to me. In other words, I do not know what proposition S is supposed to express, because I do not know the relevant meanings of several of the words in S. Hence, I cannot answer the question whether or not S (or its

---

[17] Jean-Paul Sartre, *Being and Nothingness* (New York, Philosophical Library, 1956), p. 207.

negation) expresses an unthinkable proposition. Perhaps there
is a proposition expressed by the negation of S and it is unthinkable, in which case S would be a necessary truth. On the
other hand, perhaps S and not-S express no proposition at all, in
which case it would be hard to explain why Sartre should have
written S at all. The problem of how one is to go about trying to
linguistically understand a metaphysician's statements (i.e., find
out what propositions they express, if any) is both difficult and
important. However, it is not particularly relevant to the present
essay, for I am concerned with type crossings and unthinkability,
not linguistic meaninglessness. As far as metaphysics is concerned, I can only say that perhaps the metaphysician's statements
are necessary truths, and perhaps they are empirical truths or not
truths at all. I cannot decide on them until I find out what propositions they express, and it may be some time before I do find
this out (if ever). My conclusion about the first objection, then,
is simply that it does not present any difficulty for my theory
of necessary truth. It would present a problem only if I were to
hold the view that the statements of a metaphysician do not
express necessary truths. But I do not hold this view, nor do I
see any reason why anyone should want to hold it.

The second objection has to do with a consequence of Definition B, namely, the following entailment:

C: "p is unthinkable" entails "p is necessarily false".

According to the objection, there is no reason to accept this
entailment, because there is no reason to deny that its antece-
dent ("p is unthinkable") could be true while its consequent
("p is necessarily false") is false. It is quite possible, according
to the argument, that a certain proposition should be unthinkable
even though it is only a contingent falsehood (or perhaps not
false at all, but true). Consider, for example, the following
situation.

Suppose we were to journey to another planet, and suppose
we were to discover there a race of intelligent beings different
from ourselves. It may very well be that one of the differences

between them and us is that the strange beings regard what we call "type crossings" to be only contingently false. They would say that the proposition that the theory of relativity is blue is *thinkable* and only a contingent falsehood about the world. They may say this because, instead of drawing the sort of type distinctions that we do, they draw completely different type distinctions. According to the argument, this situation would be one in which an unthinkable proposition is only contingently false. Hence, "p is unthinkable" does not entail "p is necessarily false".

My reply to this objection is that the situation presented is not properly described as a case where the proposition that the theory of relativity is blue is only contingently false. It should be described as a case where several beings utter a sentence which people have translated into English as "the proposition that the theory of relativity is blue is contingently false". But what reason is there to believe that this is an adequate translation? Furthermore, what reason is there to believe that the beings in question are right about the proposition being contingently false (if this is what they are saying), but wrong about its being thinkable? There are no reasons for any of this. Therefore, I am inclined to dismiss the objection as not having presented a genuine counter-example to my view.

However, the idea behind the objection may still persist: how can we ascertain what is true and what is false about parts of the universe which we have never observed? For example, how can we know, just by thinking, that nowhere in the universe do there exist blue theories? [18] Why should our general agreement that the existence of blue theories is unthinkable necessitate the non-existence of blue theories?

[18] It might be suggested that we know there are no blue theories because we can prove this as follows: (1) Theories are abstract entities. (2) No abstract entities are concrete entities. (3) Only concrete entities are colored. (4) Only colored entities are blue. (5) Therefore, theories are not blue. It is clear, however, that this gets us nowhere, for the question naturally arises as to how we know that premises (1)–(4) are true. Ultimately, some appeal must be made to the unthinkability of the opposite. And then we have our same problem: why should unthinkable propositions have to be false?

My answer is that we have to take what is unthinkable to be necessarily false because there is no other alternative. To say, or even to suggest in any way, the possibility of unthinkable truth (or unthinkable contingent falsehood) is necessarily to talk nonsense. Such an idea is ineffable, for we can only express that which has been apprehended by the mind (i.e., that which has been thought, and therefore is thinkable). Hence, if there is an unthinkable truth (or unthinkable contingent falsehood), it is something about which we can say nothing. But we have to take as possibilities only what we can say something about; otherwise, the notion of "possibility" could have no use. Therefore, what is unthinkable must be impossible, hence, necessarily false. In other words, we must take statement C (the entailment of "p is necessarily false" by "p is unthinkable") to be true in order to have a concept of necessity at all.

By answering the objections to Definition B, I hope to have given good reason for defining the concept of necessity (or the concept of the a priori) in terms of unthinkability. If the question is now asked "in what sense are type crossings necessarily false (or false a priori)?", I would answer: "in the sense that they express unthinkable propositions". However, this is exactly the same answer that I would give to the question "in what sense are type crossings *meaningless*?" In other words, type crossings are meaningless in exactly the same sense in which, say, mathematical falsehoods (such as "22 is divisible by 3") are meaningless.[19] To distinguish this sense of 'meaningless' from other senses of 'meaningless', such as linguistic meaninglessness, I have referred to it as "conceptual meaninglessness". Thus, a sentence is conceptually meaningless if and only if it expresses an unthinkable proposition.

We may now see the difference between sentence S (quoted

[19] Of course, as was pointed out in Section 7.1, a sense of 'meaningless' could be stipulated in which type crossings are meaningless but mathematical falsehoods are not meaningless, namely, *type meaninglessness*. But I am not concerned with this sense in the present chapter. It was Chapter 6 that attempted to deal with type meaninglessness by defining the concept of a type crossing.

above) and a type crossing such as sentence (1) ("the theory of relativity is blue"). Whereas S is linguistically meaningless to me, (1) is not linguistically meaningless to me, for, once it is given that the individual words in it are to be taken in their ordinary senses, I know perfectly well what proposition sentence (1) is supposed to express – and I see that it is indeed an unthinkable proposition. It is important to understand that the question of whether or not a sentence is conceptually meaningless cannot be answered by anyone to whom the sentence is linguistically meaningless, for such a person would not know what proposition the sentence expresses and therefore could not say whether that proposition is thinkable or unthinkable. For this reason, if I were asked whether or not sentence S is conceptually meaningless, I would have to reply that I do not know.

Since different people speak different languages and one person may not understand another's language, it is clear that linguistic meaninglessness is a subjective concept. In other words, what is linguistically meaningless to one person may not be linguistically meaningless to another. But this is not the case with conceptual meaninglessness. When a person sees a sentence to be conceptually meaningless, he knows what proposition it is supposed to express and sees that that proposition is unthinkable. There could be no point in his saying of the sentence that it is conceptually meaningless *to him*, for it is impossible for *anyone* to conceptually understand it. As long as a sentence is taken in such a way as to express an unthinkable proposition (as in the case of a type crossing), it is impossible for anyone at all to conceptually understand it. Therefore, the subjective qualifier "to so-and-so" cannot sensibly be appended to the expression 'conceptually meaningless', for in such a position it could have no use or point. Like unthinkability, in terms of which it is defined, conceptual meaninglessness is an objective concept.

AN EXTENSION OF THE TOPIC

8.1. TYPE CROSSINGS IN THE BROAD SENSE

Thus far, we have restricted type crossings to sentences which, so to speak, cross types of *things*. We have not considered sentences which cross other kinds of types, such as types of activities and types of properties.

Yet, there are sequences of words which could perhaps fit the latter description. For example, consider sequences (20) and (21), which are as follows:

(20) Jones saw the book carefully.
(21) The package is brightly large.

It could be said, with respect to (20), that seeing is not the type of activity that can be done carefully, that only voluntary or intentional activities can be done carefully. And with respect to (21), it perhaps might be said that being large is not the type of property that could be qualified as brightly, that the only properties which could be thus qualified are those which are derived from activities (such as being decorated, being colored, being painted, etc.).[1] This suggests the possibility of defining a new concept of type crossing, one which would include not only all those sentences which we have called "simple type crossings", but sequences such as (20) and (21) as well. Let us label this concept "type crossings in the broad sense", or "type

---

[1] The term 'activity' is here being used in the broadest possible sense, including even states of being. Thus, glowing is to be regarded as an "activity" of the candle. As will be pointed out later, it is more natural to express the distinction appealed to here in the formal mode of speech, that is, to say "an adjective derived from a verb" rather than "a property derived from an activity".

crossings$_b$." for short. This, then, is our first problem: how might the expression 'type crossing$_b$' be defined?

As a first stab, let us consider the following definition:

Definition D: A type crossing$_b$ is a sequence of words which says of one type of proposition factor something that has application only to another type of proposition factor.

The term 'proposition factor' (borrowed from Ryle's article "Categories") is supposed to designate anything that might be a possible value of a variable in a propositional function (of any order whatever). Thus, it stands for things, activities, states of being, properties, relations, and whatever else might be designated by nouns, verbs, or adjectives.

One main objection to Definition D is that it is too inclusive, for it would include as type crossings$_b$ not only sequences which cross types, but sequences which cross kinds of types. For example, consider the following sequence:

(86) Scientists truth the universe.

In order to convert (86) into an intelligible[2] sentence, the noun 'truth' must be replaced by a verb (e.g., 'study'). In other

---

[2] In his article "Semi-sentences" (printed in *The Structure of Language,* edited by Fodor & Katz, Englewood Cliffs, Prentice-Hall, Inc., 1964, p. 402), Jerrold J. Katz claims of this sequence that it is comprehensible to speakers of English. Now, it is no doubt true that *some* speakers might give it a metaphorical or elliptical interpretation in terms of which they could understand it, but it seems unlikely that a large majority of speakers would be inclined to do this. In any case, it is clear that, taken literally, the sequence is nonsensical. It is of interest to note that Katz's concept of "semi-sentence" is in a certain respect diametrically opposed to my concept of "type crossing". Whereas type crossings are grammatical, semi-sentences are ungrammatical (or at best semi-grammatical). And whereas type crossings are *meaningless* by virtue of the *literal* interpretations given to their key words, semi-sentences are *meaningful* by virtue of the *non-literal* interpretations given to their key words. In brief, whereas type crossings are grammatical though meaningless, semi-sentences are meaningful though ungrammatical (or semi-grammatical). Needless to say, the theoretical problems presented by type crossings are altogether different from those presented by semi-sentences.

words, a thing (one kind of type) must be replaced by an activity (another kind of type). Another sequence to illustrate this point is the following:

(87) Eat admires sincerity.

Here, it is a verb (or activity) that needs to be replaced by a noun (or thing). Both (86) and (87) are too deviant to be regarded as type crossings at all (even as type crossings$_b$). To include them would be to include just about any string of words at all. For example, "runs drinks jump" could be transformed into "Jones drinks beer" (by replacement of nouns for verbs) or into "Jones is tall" or into practically any three word sentence. Thus, Definition D must be ruled out as being too inclusive.

Perhaps we could abandon the attempt to define 'type crossing$_b$' directly and put forward a series of definitions, one for each kind of type. Thus, our original working definition of a type crossing could be taken as a rough definition of a "thing type crossing". Then the definition of an "activity type crossing" could go as follows:

An activity type crossing is a sequence which says of one type of activity something that has application only to a different type of activity.

An example of an activity type crossing would be sequence (20), which says of an involuntary activity (viz., seeing) something (namely, that it is done carefully) that has application only to a different type of activity (viz., voluntary or intentional activities). In a similar way, a definition could be put forward for "property type crossings" (exemplified by sequence (21)), and perhaps for other kinds of type crossings as well. We could then define a type crossing$_b$ as any member of any of the classes defined in the given way. Let us refer to this as the "series approach" to type crossings$_b$, since it involves putting forward a series of definitions.

There are a number of minor objections to the series approach that need to be taken up. One objection is that it excludes certain sequences which ought to be classified as type crossings$_b$, such as the following:

(88) He stated, seasoned, rode, and cautioned it.

Since there is no way to construe (88) as saying of one type of activity something that has application only to a different type of activity, it seems that there is no way for (88) to be classified as a type crossing$_b$. To this objection it may be replied that, although sequences such as (88) involve some sort of crossing of types, they are too complex to be included under any definition of type crossings$_b$. That is, they bear the same relation to type crossings$_b$ as sentence (46) ("that thing is both a prime number and green") bears to simple thing type crossings. Thus, they may perhaps be called "complex type crossings$_b$". Whether or not it is possible to construct a precise theory of complex type crossings$_b$ is a question I shall not attempt to answer in the present essay. In any case, there is clearly a difference between (88) and sequences such as (20), and also between (88) and sequences such as (86). It may well be that both of these differences could be taken account of by classifying (88) as a "complex type crossing$_b$", even though this expression cannot be defined in any precise way.

Another sort of sequence which might be relegated to the class of complex type crossings$_b$ is that in which there are at least two different crossings of different kinds of types. This is illustrated by the following two sequences:

(89) A brightly heavy number is valid.
(90) Jones carefully knew that the package is brightly large.

Once these are admitted as complex type crossings$_b$, the door would be open to other sequences of unlimited complexity. Consider, for example:

(91) My virtuous horizon's vehemently fishing telephone brightly extricates makeshift brawny flashbacks.

Jumbled as (89)–(91) are, they are still, in an important way, more grammatical than (86) and (87), for they only cross types; they do not cross kinds of types.

A second objection to the series approach is that there seems to be no reason why "conjunction type crossings" could not be included in the series. For example, consider the following sequence:

(92) Jack but Jill went up the hill.

Is (92) to be called a type crossing$_b$? Surely this would be stretching the concept too far. If we include (92) as a type crossing$_b$, then we would also have to include such word salad as sequence (26) ("Smith although Jones spoke until not Brown"), which was discussed on page 46. It is clear that we do not want to extend the term 'type crossing$_b$' to cover such sequences. Yet, it is not clear how the series approach is to be handled so as to prevent such an extension. To simply limit the series in such a way as to exclude "conjunction type crossings" seems too arbitrary. Some theoretical principle needs to be introduced in order to justify such a limitation.

Another way to put the objection would be to point out that unless some principle is formulated to indicate exactly what kinds of type crossings$_b$ are to be defined, it will not be possible to use the series approach to show of a given sequence that it is *not* a type crossing$_b$. For example, how could it ever be shown of sequence (24) ("he is have were") that it is not a type crossing$_b$? After all, (24) *can* be converted into a meaningful sentence (e.g., "he may have come") simply by substitution of verbs for verbs. This, in itself, is some indication that it might be a type crossing$_b$. It seems, then, that the series approach must be spelled out much more fully (or else abandoned completely in favor of some other theory) in order to guarantee the exclusion of such sequences as (24) and (26) from the class of type crossings$_b$.

I do not intend in the present book to work out a theory of type crossings$_b$ which would meet these objections. I merely present the area as one into which our topic naturally extends and on which further work needs to be done. However, I *would* like to take up the philosophical question of the ultimate basis of the meaninglessness (or oddity) of type crossings$_b$. This question will be seen to have important connections with the corresponding question in the case of "thing type crossings".

8.2. THE PHILOSOPHICAL QUESTION EXTENDED

In the absence of any precise theory of type crossings$_b$, it seems the only practicable way to approach the philosophical question is in terms of specific examples. Let us take sequences (20) and (21) as clear cases of type crossings$_b$. Then we need to raise the following questions with respect to each of them:

(a) Is the sequence a necessary falsehood?
(b) Is it conceptually meaningless?
(c) Does it express an unthinkable proposition?
(d) Is it at best only semi-grammatical?
(e) Does it violate type-rules?

With respect to questions (a)–(c), I am inclined to answer "yes", though my inclination is not so strong here as it is in the case of type crossings in the narrow sense (i.e., "thing type crossings"). With respect to questions (d) and (e), my inclination to answer "yes" is stronger in the case of (20) and (21) than in the case of thing type crossings. Therefore, I *shall* put forward a qualified "yes" for (d) and (e) as well as for (a)–(c).

An immediate objection would be to point out that giving an affirmative answer to all five questions is inconsistent with the positions expressed in previous chapters. For example, in Sections 3.3 and 3.4, it was argued that since type crossings are false, they must be grammatical and not merely semi-grammatical. This suggests that it would be inconsistent to answer both question (a) and question (d) affirmatively. Furthermore, in Section 3.4 it was argued that there is no precise criterion for degree of grammaticality, and in Chapter 4 it was argued that type-rules are not in effect in ordinary language. To give an affirmative answer to questions (d) and (e) seems to run counter to these earlier results. In what follows, I shall attempt to justify my affirmative answers and also to qualify those answers in such a way as to make them compatible with the positions taken in previous chapters.

Let us begin with question (a). Are sequences (20) and (21) necessary falsehoods? I want to argue that there is sufficient reason to regard them as such because their negations ("Jones did not see the book carefully" and "the package is not brightly large") can be proved true by appeal to a priori premises alone. The proofs, which are patterned after Proofs A-C of Chapter 2, would go as follows:

Proof D
(1) Jones's seeing the book was a case of seeing.
(2) Seeing is not a voluntary or intentional activity.
(3) Only voluntary or intentional activities can be done carefully.
(4) Therefore, Jones's seeing the book was not done carefully.
(5) Therefore, Jones did not see the book carefully.

Proof E
(1) The package's being large is a case of being large.
(2) Being large is a property, but not a property which is derived from an activity.
(3) The only properties that can be qualified as brightly are those which are derived from activities.
(4) Therefore, the package's being large cannot be qualified as brightly.
(5) Therefore, the package is not brightly large.

Proof E strikes me as more awkward than Proof D, mainly because its steps (3) and (4) have the ring of ungrammaticality. However, it may be that this awkwardness could be eliminated by an improved formulation. In any case, there does not seem to be anything objectionable about the idea of drawing a distinction between two classes of properties, those which can be qualified as "brightly" and those which cannot. By appeal to such a distinction, it can be argued that being large is not the type of property that can be qualified as "brightly", and hence, there is at least some point in classifying sequence (21) as necessarily false.

Given that sequences (20) and (21) are necessary falsehoods, it follows, by virtue of the considerations raised in Section 7.5, that they are conceptually meaningless and designate unthinkable propositions. Once an affirmative answer is granted to question (a), I cannot see that there could be any basis for denying an affirmative answer to questions (b) and (c) as well. It is question (a) that is most troublesome, and much of the trouble lies in the fact that Proofs D and E seem unnatural and inappropriate (especially Proof E). It might plausibly be argued that such proofs (or proofs analogous to them) should be expressed in the formal mode of speech rather than in the material mode of speech. The formal mode of speech is meta-linguistic speech, that is, speech which has as its subject matter linguistic expressions, phrases, sentences, etc. The material mode of speech is speech which is about things, activities, properties, etc. If we were to express proofs analogous to D and E in the formal mode of speech, they would go as follows:

Proof D'
(1) In the sequence "Jones saw the book carefully", the verb 'to see' is modified by the adverb 'carefully'.
(2) The verb 'to see' is not an intentional verb.
(3) Only intentional verbs can be meaningfully modified by the adverb 'carefully'.
(4) Therefore, the sequence "Jones saw the book carefully" is meaningless.

Proof E'
(1) In the sequence "the package is brightly large", the adjective 'large' is modified by the adverb 'brightly'.
(2) The adjective 'large' is not derived from a verb.

(3) The only adjectives that can be meaningfully modified by the adverb 'brightly' are those which are derived from verbs.
(4) Therefore, the sequence "the package is brightly large" is meaningless.

It is to be noted that these proofs have quite different conclusions from those of D and E. The appeal to the formal mode of speech cannot establish the falsity of type crossings$_b$; it can only establish their meaninglessness. But what is this sense of 'meaningless'? It is not conceptual meaninglessness but *syntactic* meaninglessness. Sequences which are meaningless in this sense are at best only semi-grammatical.

It does make sense to speak of one sequence as being "more grammatical than" another sequence. For example, I would say that "the theory of relativity is blue" is more grammatical than "the package is brightly large", which, in turn, is more grammatical than "the theory is but". However, despite the efforts of Noam Chomsky, I do not believe that the concept of degree of grammaticality can be given a definition which is both precise and adequate. On the contrary, it is a concept that can be applied only in an intuitive way. Nevertheless, it does make sense to distinguish semi-grammatical sequences, such as (20) and (21), from sequences of words which are completely ungrammatical (such as "is were he if"). This conception of sequences (20) and (21) as semi-grammatical can be expressed, in part, by Proofs D' and E', and by talking about them in the formal mode of speech.

Now, what about the charge of inconsistency? How can I maintain, in light of the arguments of Sections 3.3 and 3.4, that sequences (20) and (21) are necessary falsehoods (as established by Proofs D and E) and also that they are syntactically meaningless (as established by Proofs D' and E') and, hence, at best only semi-grammatical? My answer is that it is possible to regard (or interpret) the sequences from either of two points of view. These may be referred to as "the material point of view" and "the formal point of view". When we regard (20) from the material point of view, we are inclined to say that seeing is not the type of activity that can be done carefully and that therefore (20) is necessarily false (or is conceptually meaningless or designates an unthinkable proposition). On the other hand, when we regard (20) from the formal point of view, we are inclined to say that the verb 'to see' is not the type of verb that can be modified by the adverb 'carefully', and that therefore (20) is syntactically meaningless (or syntactically ill-formed) and at best only semi-grammatical. These same remarks are applicable to sequence (21). When we regard (21) from the material point of view, we are inclined to say that being large is not the type of property that can be qualified as brightly, and that therefore (21) is necessarily false (or is conceptually meaningless or designates an unthinkable proposition). On the other hand, when we regard (21) from the formal point of view, we are inclined to say that the adjective 'large' is not the type of adjective that can be modified by the adverb 'brightly', and that therefore (21) is syntactically meaningless (or syntactically ill-formed) and at best only semi-grammatical.

If we adopt the formal point of view with respect to (20) and (21), then we could, from that point of view, not only answer question (d) affirmatively, but also question (e). In other words, we could take the type-rules in question to be the grammatical rules infringed by (20) and (21). Such rules may more plausibly be claimed to be in effect in ordinary language than the corresponding rules in the case of thing type crossings.

Thus, my answer to the question "what is the ultimate basis of the meaninglessness of sequences (20) and (21)?" is as follows. We can interpret these sequences in either of two ways, from the material point of view and from the formal point of view. If we regard them from the material point of view, then we regard them as being *conceptually* meaningless. On the other hand, if we regard them from the formal point of view, then we regard them as being *syntactically* meaningless (or ill-formed). In the former case, the ultimate basis of their (conceptual) meaninglessness lies in the fact that the propositions which they designate are unthinkable. In the latter case, the ultimate basis of their (syntactic) meaninglessness lies in the fact that they violate certain rules of grammar and are therefore at best only semi-grammatical. My own inclination is to regard the material point of view to be more natural and plausible in the case of (20), and the formal point of view to be more natural and plausible in the case of (21). This inclination will be defended shortly.

A fundamental objection may at this point be lodged against the whole tenor of the book. It is an objection which is based on the approach to philosophy and science expressed in the writings of Rudolph Carnap. Here is an excerpt from those writings:

> The fact that, in philosophical writings – even in those which are free from metaphysics – obscurities so frequently arise, and that in philosophical discussions people so often find themselves talking at cross purposes, is in large part due to the use of the material instead of the formal mode of speech. The habit of formulating in the material mode of speech causes us, in the first place, to deceive ourselves about the objects of our own investigations: pseudo-object-sentences mislead us into thinking that we are dealing with extra-linguistic objects such as numbers, things, properties, experiences, states of affairs, space, time, and so on; and the fact that, in reality, it is a case of language and its connections (such as numerical expressions, thing-designations, spatial co-ordinates, etc.) is disguised from us by the material mode of speech. This fact only becomes clear by translation into the formal mode of speech, or, in other words, into syntactical sentences about language and linguistic expressions.[3]

The objection based on this outlook is that the appeal to the material mode of speech in discussing type crossings only results in confusion. This confusion is revealed in the awkwardness of Proofs D and E, as well as in the difficulties inherent in the appeal to unthinkability. On the other hand, when type crossings are discussed solely in the formal mode of speech, the result, according to this outlook, is nothing but clarity and illumination.

---

[3] Rudolph Carnap, *The Logical Syntax of Language* (New York, The Humanities Press, 1937), pp. 298-299. Carnap goes on to illustrate, at great length, the translation of the material mode of speech into the formal mode of speech. It would be foolish to question the usefulness of this procedure for many areas of philosophy and science.

Therefore, the material point of view ought to be abandoned altogether in the interpretation and discussion of type crossings, whether they be thing type crossings or whether they be other sorts of type crossings$_b$.

Much has already been said in reply to this objection, especially in Chapters 3 and 4. However, the question does need to be raised as to what determines the point of view from which we ought to regard a given sequence. On what grounds, for instance, do I completely exclude the formal point of view from the discussion of thing type crossings? In reply to this, two main factors need to be cited.

First of all, there are the proofs: the proof of the negation of the given sequence, constructed in the material mode of speech, and the proof that the sequence is syntactically meaningless, constructed in the formal mode of speech. Let us refer to these as "the material proof" and "the formal proof", respectively. Proofs A-E would be examples of material proofs, and Proofs D' and E' would be examples of formal proofs. We need to ask these questions: "Is the material proof awkward? Does it contain steps which are themselves syntactically meaningless? Does it sound implausible?" In my opinion, of the five material proofs, A-E, only Proof E turns out unsatisfactory with respect to these criteria. The other four should receive at least a passing (or satisfactory) rating. Now, in addition to the material proof with respect to a given sequence, the corresponding formal proof should also be evaluated. We need to ask: "Is the formal proof artificial? Does it appeal to invented *ad hoc* classifications? Does it sound implausible?" On these criteria, Proof E' fares much better than Proof D'. In Proof D' an appeal is made to "intentional verbs", which is an artificial and invented classification. The corresponding appeal in Proof E', to adjectives which are derived from verbs, seems much more proper. Whereas Proof D seems less artificial and more plausible than Proof D', Proof E is more artificial and less plausible than Proof E'.

The question should now be raised as to the formal proofs which would correspond to Proofs A-C. Actually, we have a guide in this matter in the person of Max Black, a foremost advocate of the appeal to the formal mode of speech in philosophy, as opposed to the material mode of speech. In his paper "Comments on Arthur Pap's 'Types and Meaninglessness' ",[4] Black says the following:

> I am not convinced that a proof of the meaninglessness of "Socrates is a prime number" must use the statement, *Socrates is not a natural number*, as a premiss. An appropriate pattern of argument seems to be the following: 'Socrates' is a personal name; 'is a prime number' is an arithmetical predicate; and the combination of a personal name and an arithmetical predicate is senseless. Hence, "Socrates is a prime number" is senseless. This seems to me the kind of proof that is needed, yet it uses no statement about the man *Socrates* (or about the class of men) as a premiss. The expressions, 'is a personal name' and 'is an arithmetical predicate', correspond to what Mr. Pap calls "type predicates". Unlike him, however, I have taken these expressions to stand for kinds of *expressions*, not kinds of *things*, such as men or natural numbers. I think Russell was right when he said: "The theory of types is really a theory of symbols, not of things".

Using this guide, we may formulate the formal proofs which would correspond to Proofs A-C as follows:

Proof A'
(1) The noun phrase 'the theory of relativity' is an abstract noun phrase rather than a concrete noun phrase.
(2) Only concrete noun phrases can be meaningfully combined with color predicates such as 'is blue'.
(3) Therefore, the sequence "the theory of relativity is blue" is meaningless.

Proof B'
(1) The noun 'smells' is an olfactory noun.
(2) Olfactory nouns cannot meaningfully be combined with auditory predicates such as 'are loud'.
(3) Therefore, the sequence "smells are loud" is meaningless.

---

[4]   This is the paper which was read at the December 1957 meeting of the American Philosophical Association, Eastern Division, as part of a symposium with Arthur Pap.

Proof C'
(1) The noun phrase 'moral perfection' is state noun phrase.
(2) State noun phrases cannot meaningfully be combined with arithmetical predicates such as 'is a prime number'.
(3) Therefore, the sequence "moral perfection is a prime number" is meaningless.

These proofs appeal to such linguistic classifications as 'abstract noun phrase', 'concrete noun phrase', 'color predicate', 'olfactory noun', 'auditory predicate', 'state noun phrase', and 'arithmetical predicate'. Yet, none of these are classifications employed by grammarians. Some of them are artificial to a ridiculous extent, such as 'olfactory noun' and 'auditory predicate'. For these reasons, Proofs A'-C' strike me as artificial and as less plausible than their material counterparts.

The main factor determining whether a proof is awkward and artificial is the kind of types to which appeal is made in the proof. Types can be classified in the material mode of speech as to whether they are types of things, types of activities, types of properties, etc. or in the formal mode of speech as to whether they are types of nouns (or noun phrases), types of verbs, types of adjectives, types of predicates, etc. For some of these kinds of types, only the classification in the formal mode is natural and plausible. For example, consider *conjunctions,* as opposed to their material counterparts, which perhaps might be called "connections" (not to be confused with relations, or multi-placed properties). It is much more natural to classify conjunctions as to types than to classify "connections" as to types. It is largely for this reason that it would be quite natural and plausible to regard "conjunction type crossings" (if we were to admit such a notion) from the formal point of view. For example, to regard sequence (92) ("Jack but Jill went up the hill") from the material point of view and thereby maintain that it expresses an unthinkable proposition (saying of one type of "connection" something that has application only to another type of "connection") would be highly ridiculous. On the contrary, thinkability and unthinkability both presuppose a high degree of grammaticality. The more plausible it is to regard a sequence from the formal point of view, the less plausible it is to regard it from the material point of view. In the case of "conjunction type crossings", the formal point of view is so plausible that the material point of view becomes ridiculous. The reason for this, basically, is that conjunctions are strictly structure words rather than content words. A word must have some content (as nouns, verbs, and adjectives do) in order for it, or what it designates, to be plausibly regarded from the material point of view.

Unlike conjunctions, in the case of nouns, verbs, and adjectives, it is always a pertinent question to ask whether the type to which an appeal is made is more plausibly regarded from the material point of view or from the formal point of view. Consider, for example, the class of properties which are derived from activities (material mode) as opposed to the class of adjectives which are derived from verbs (formal mode). Here, the formal point of view is more plausible because the sort of derivation that is meant is a purely grammatical derivation. It is a strictly grammatical point that the past participle of most verbs can be used as an adjective. That is why steps (2) and (3) of Proof E' are less awkward and more natural than the corresponding steps in Proof E. The type involved here is more plausibly regarded as a formal type (a type of adjective) than as a material type (a type of property).

However, suppose we consider the class of intentional activities (material mode) as opposed to the class of intentional verbs (formal mode). Here, it is the material point of view which is the more plausible, because the distinction between intentional and unintentional (or voluntary and involuntary) is not a grammatical or linguistic distinction. So, the type involved is more plausibly regarded as a material type (a type of activity) than as a formal type (a type of verb). That is why steps (2) and (3) of Proof D are less awkward and artificial than the corresponding steps in Proof D'. And that is why it is more plausible to regard sequence (20) from the material point of view than from the formal point of view. These same considerations apply to the kinds of types appealed to in Proofs A-C and Proofs A'-C'. In each case, the material type is less awkward and less artificial than the corresponding formal type. And that is one of the reasons why the type crossings whose negations are proved by Proofs A-C are far more plausibly regarded from the material point of view than from the formal point of view. But I do not consider this the main reason.

It is the second main factor determining the point of view from which we ought to regard a given sequence that is perhaps the more important. This is the question of the strength of the argument from missing conditions and the argument from non-linguistic response with respect to the given sequence. In Chapter 4, the arguments from missing conditions and non-linguistic response were presented with respect to the thing type crossing "the theory of relativity is blue". But perhaps the arguments would not be as sound or as strong with respect to other kinds of type crossings$_b$. I would say that the plausibility of the appeal to the material point of view is determined mainly by the strength of these two arguments relative to the given sequence. This, then, is my main reason for appealing exclusively to the material point of view in the case of thing type crossings: the fact that the arguments from missing conditions and non-linguistic response are so overwhelmingly strong in their case.

Let us now consider the application of these arguments to sequences (20) and (21). The argument from missing conditions is that the type-rules corresponding to the given sequences, however they may be formulated, are not in effect in ordinary language for the reason that there is no practice of violation and correction with respect to such rules. And the reason for this is that the conditions for such correction, namely, that sequences (20) and (21) be taken both as embodying linguistic mistakes and also as being type crossings$_b$, never in fact obtain.

The argument from non-linguistic response is that even if the conditions for correction were to obtain, there would still be no tendency on the part of the listener (our "Smith" of Chapter 4) to appeal to anything like rules of language in his correction.

I believe that the argument from missing conditions is sound when applied to (20) and (21). To bring this out, let us use the example of Smith and Jones again. In order to take Jones's utterance of one of these sequences as a type crossing$_b$, Smith must suppose Jones to mean by his words what is normally meant by them. It is part of the concept of a "type crossing" that the individual words in it be taken literally and in their usual senses. (See page 12.) But then Jones would not be taken to be making a linguistic mistake. Rather, if his utterance is taken as a type crossing, then it seems that the only way for Smith to interpret the situation is by regarding Jones as not being serious (or perhaps as providing an example of something, etc.). Thus, even with respect to sequences such as (20) and (21), the conditions for correction on the basis of type-rules never do arise in ordinary discourse.

But when we turn to the argument from non-linguistic response, the situation is somewhat different. We are now to suppose that the conditions for correction by appeal to type-rules *were* to arise. That is, on the basis of careful questioning, Smith is able to rule out all the normal interpretations of Jones's utterance so that the only possibility left is that Jones really is *asserting* a type crossing$_b$ and is presumably making a mistake thereby. In the case of thing type crossings, it was argued that even under such conditions, Smith would still have no tendency whatever to appeal to language or linguistic conventions in his reaction. But in the case of sequences such as (20) and (21), this is not so.

It is important to understand just what is at issue here. In Smith's questioning of Jones, it is assumed that he is able to rule out all interpretations according to which Jones is using his words in an elliptical or unusual way. For example, in the case of sequence (20), it is established that when Jones says "see carefully" he does not mean "look at carefully" or "examine carefully" or anything of that sort. Indeed, if he were to mean something of that sort, then his utterance would not be a type crossing at all. Whether or not it is a type crossing depends on how *he* interprets it. We are assuming that, on the basis of his questioning, Smith is able to establish that when Jones says "see carefully", he really means "see carefully" and, furthermore, he *knows* perfectly well what 'see' means and what 'carefully' means. Thus, his utterance really *is* a type crossing$_b$. What I want to maintain is that in these very odd circumstances, Smith's reaction to Jones's utterances *would* probably include an appeal to language or linguistic conventions. And so, the argument from non-linguistic response, though effective with respect to thing type crossings, is not so effective with respect to activity type crossings (such as (20)) and property type crossings (such as (21)). Nevertheless, all this is a matter of degree (or probability). The tendency of the listener to appeal to language in his reaction (or the probability that he would appeal to language in his reaction) would vary from type crossing$_b$ to type crossing$_b$. I am inclined to believe that this tendency would be greater in the case of (21) than in the case of (20), and that this is further reason to regard (21) from the formal point of view. Sequence (20), on the other hand, is more or less on the borderline.[5] It is to some extent natural to regard it from the formal point of view (certainly much more so than in the case of thing type crossings), but I still consider it more natural to regard it from the material point of view, especially in light of the application of the first factor to it.

One might wonder how the premises of the argument from non-linguistic response could ever be experimentally verified. As I indicated in the preface to this book, my general method is theoretical rather than descriptive or experimental. However, in the particular area of the argument from non-linguistic re-

---

[5] This does not at all entail that the proposition designated by (20) is on a borderline between thinkability and unthinkability. On the contrary, if (20) is regarded from the material point of view. then the proposition it designates is *definitely* unthinkable. What is meant, rather, is that the proportion of people who would regard (20) from the material point of view is only slightly greater than the proportion of people who would regard it from the formal point of view.

sponse, I may appear to be relying on observations of linguistic behavior. Actually, this is not the case. Such observations are not even possible because the conditions for them (as shown by the argument from missing conditions) never in fact arise. For this reason, the premises of the argument from non-linguistic response are *not* verifiable, and thus, the argument, instead of being based on actual observations, is really based on highly theoretical or hypothetical suppositions. On the other hand, any discussion of type-rules on the level in question *must* be of this nature since such rules are never in fact appealed to in ordinary language. Certainly, *my* appeal to the highly theoretical suppositions mentioned is not any more questionable than that of the defender of the linguistic approach to type crossings. Just as I have done, so also, he too must appeal to such tenuous considerations as how a person *would* react *if* certain conditions (which do not in fact obtain) *were* to obtain. In this respect, his method is no less suspect than mine, as far as verifiability is concerned.

This completes my discussion of the two factors which determine the point of view from which we ought to regard a given sequence. I hope to have explained why thing type crossings should be regarded solely from a material point of view, whereas, in the case of other kinds of type crossings$_b$ (with the exception of such oddities as "conjunction type crossings", if they are admitted as type crossings$_b$ at all), it is an open question which point of view to adopt. I suggested reasons why sequence (20) would be more naturally regarded from a material point of view, while (21) would be more naturally regarded from a formal point of view.

And finally, on the question whether an affirmative answer to all five questions, (a)–(e), is possible, I would say that it is possible, but only in the following sense. When the given sequence is regarded from the material point of view, questions (a)–(c) may be given an affirmative answer, while questions (d) and (e) would in that case be answered negatively. And when the sequence is regarded from the formal point of view, questions (d) and (e) may be given an affirmative answer, in which case questions (a)–(c) would not even arise (since they all *pre-suppose* a negative answer to (d) and (e)). So, although an affirmative answer can be given to all five questions with respect to the same sequence, it cannot be given from the same point of view. It would be quite inconsistent to answer all five questions "yes" with respect to a given sequence regarded from the same point of view, whether it be the material point of view or the formal point of view. In this way, my results with respect to type crossings$_b$ are made compatible with my earlier results with respect to thing type crossings.

There is one other service performed by this discussion of the two factors determining point of view, and that is to show that the choice of point of view is not arbitrary. If one were to think that the choice is arbitrary, he might be inclined to argue as follows. The thinkability approach to type crossings is not essentially different from the linguistic approach, which was rejected in Chapters 3 and 4. It is simply a difference in mode of expression. The thinkability approach employs the material mode of speech and the linguistic approach employs the formal mode of speech. But they say essentially the same thing. One's choice of approach is determined by his choice of mode of speech. And his choice of mode of speech is ultimately arbitrary. Therefore, the difference between the thinkability approach and the linguistic approach is ultimately arbitrary, depending simply upon one's terminological preferences.

In reply to this argument, I shall maintain that one's choice of mode of speech is not arbitrary. There are very definite criteria which determine the appropriateness of a given mode of speech with respect to a given sequence. And these are the two factors which I have just presented. I would agree that *if* the thinkability approach and the linguistic approach could both be adequately defended, then they must be merely terminological variations of each other. However, I deny that they can both be adequately defended. By appeal to the two factors, it can be ascertained that with respect to thing type crossings, the formal mode of speech is definitely inappropriate, and therefore my rejection of the linguistic approach in Chapters 3 and 4 was quite justified. In this respect, only the thinkability approach can be defended in the case of thing type crossings; the linguistic approach is refutable. Thus, if the thinkability approach is correct, then the linguistic approach must be incorrect.

9

RECAPITULATION AND FINAL REMARKS

In Chapter 2, it was argued that type crossings are synthetic a priori falsehoods. They are falsehoods because their negations can be proved true; they are a priori because the proofs in question contain only a priori premises; and they are synthetic because there is no way to derive contradictions from them by appeal to conventional definitions. Two questions were raised: "what distinguishes type crossings from other synthetic a priori falsehoods such as sentences (14)–(16)?" and "what is the ultimate basis of their meaninglessness?" In Chapters 3 and 4, it was argued that the answers to these questions do not lie in the concepts of ungrammaticality (or semi-grammaticality) or violation of type-rules.

In Chapters 5 and 6, the question pursued was: "what is a type crossing?" In Chapter 5, two theories of type crossings were examined and rejected, and in Chapter 6, a new approach to the topic was undertaken. First, a distinction was drawn between simple type crossings and complex type crossings. Very roughly, a simple type crossing is a sentence which ascribes to something, x, a property with which the type associated is a class to which x does not belong. And a complex type crossing, very roughly, is a sentence whose translation into the language of symbolic logic applies to a variable two properties at least one of which has associated with it a type none of whose members has the other property. Since both of these definitions employ the concept of the type associated with a given property, that concept had to be defined in order for the theory of type crossings to be complete. It was found that the type associated with an accidental property could be defined simply as the class of things which can thinkably have that property. However, this sort of definition would not work in the case of the type associated with an essential property, because *all* false ascriptions of essential properties are unthinkable, including sentences (such as (15)) which are not type crossings. An attempt was made to define "type associated with an essential property" in terms of the concept of a subject matter, but this ran into insuperable difficulties and had to be abandoned. The approach finally settled upon was the "genus-definition" approach, a hodgepodge of criteria which was put forward, not so much because there is any great assurance behind it, as because it does not suffer from any very obvious difficulties and because there do not seem to be any alternatives to it. Whether the genus-definition approach proves to be an adequate theory of essential type crossings must be left to the future to decide.

In Chapter 7, it was pointed out that a sense of 'meaningless' may be stipulated in which type crossings are meaningless but other a priori falsehoods (such as (14)–(16)) are not meaningless. I referred to this as "type meaninglessness". As it turns out, the concept of type meaninglessness is the same as the concept of being a type crossing. So, the question "what is the ultimate basis of the type meaninglessness of type crossings?" is equivalent to the question "what is a type crossing?" and is thus answered by the theory of type crossings put forward in Chapter 6, namely, by the thinkability approach in the case of accidental type crossings and by the genus-definition approach in the case of essential type crossings.

The main question pursued in Chapter 7, however, was that of the ultimate basis of the *conceptual* meaninglessness of type crossings (i.e., that sense of 'meaningless' in which a sentence is meaningless if and only if we cannot understand what it would be like for it to be true). The answer given to this question was that type crossings are conceptually meaningless for the same reason that all necessary (or a priori) falsehoods are conceptually meaningless, namely, they express combinations of concepts that are unthinkable (i.e., that cannot be put together in thought). This notion of unthinkability was explored and defended at great length in Chapter 7. And the limits of its application were further defined in Chapter 8, where the problem was extended to kinds of type crossings other than those previously considered.

The answer to the question of conceptual meaninglessness may be divided into two parts, a negative thesis and a positive thesis. These may be expressed as follows:

(I): The basis of the conceptual meaninglessness (or necessary falsity) of type crossings does not lie in their violation of conventions of ordinary language.

(II): Rather, it lies in the unthinkability of the combinations of concepts which they express.

The negative thesis, namely (I), is based on the results of Chapters 2, 3, and 4, in which it was shown that type crossings do not violate definitional conventions, grammatical conventions, or type conventions. The positive thesis, namely (II), is based on arguments put forward in Chapter 7, and also in parts of Chapters 5, 6, and 8. Now, before the book is concluded, perhaps some remarks of a general sort are in order.

It should be pointed out, first of all, that there are two ways to defend thesis (I). The way it was defended in the book was to argue that type crossings do not violate any conventions of ordinary language. However, another way is to argue that even if type crossings were to violate such conventions, that would still not be the basis of their conceptual meaninglessness. Suppose, for example, that at some time in the future, type-rules are formulated and taught to children just as rules of grammar and punctuation are taught to them now. In that case, type-rules would become explicit rules of ordinary language, and would indeed be violated by type crossings. But thesis (II) would still be true; for what would be the basis of those rules? What would guide the person who formulates them? It would be the unthinkability of the propositions expressed by type crossings. in a sense, the rules would be formulated in order to eliminate from language what is already eliminated from thought. Therefore, they would be of no significance, theoretical or practical. And so they would not be the basis of the conceptual meaninglessness (or necessary falsity) of type crossings. That basis would still lie in the unthink-ability of the propositions expressed by type crossings, whether type-rules are made a part of language or not.

As was pointed out on page 72, even if type-rules *are* in effect in ordinary language and always have been, they would still not help us understand the nature of type crossings. That written declarative sentences cannot end in a question mark is a matter of convention. But that theories cannot be blue is not a matter of convention. If it were, then we ought to know what it would be like for the convention to be different, just as we can know what it would be like to finish a written declarative sentence with a question mark. However, we cannot know what it would be like for a theory to be blue. The concept of a theory and the concept of being blue just do not "fit" together. And this is a fact about the concepts, not about man's rules and conventions. It would be true that theories cannot be blue no matter what man's conventions are; it would be true even if the human race never existed. Thus, even if ordinary language were to contain an explicit linguistic rule to the effect that only spatially extended things can be said to be blue, it would prove nothing. Such a rule would be completely superfluous and pointless (like telling someone to use only meaningful expressions when trying to com-municate). Even if language did contain such conventions, the basis of the conceptual meaninglessness (and necessary falsity) of type crossings would still lie in the unthinkability of the propo-sitions they express – i.e., in the fact that they contain concepts which just do not "fit" together. Therefore, I would still want to defend my positive thesis, (II), and there would be no incon-sistency in my doing so.

Another general point is that although thesis (II) entails thesis (I) (as indicated at the very end of Chapter 8), (I) does not entail (II). It is possible for (I) to be true and (II) false. But to what alternative could we turn in that case? Is there some third answer to the question about conceptual meaninglessness in addi-tion to the appeal to linguistic conventions and the appeal to un-thinkability? It seems not. At least I cannot think of any *third answer*. However, there is a third approach to the topic which might appropriately (though I shall not defend this) be called "the Wittgensteinian approach" (i.e., the approach that the followers of Ludwig Wittgenstein might take). It is the approach whereby the question itself is rejected as meaningless or unanswerable. This possibility was discussed briefly on pages 140-141.

The way to defend this Wittgensteinian approach would be to attack the other two approaches. Since I have already provided grounds for rejecting the linguistic approach, all that would need to be shown is that the unthinkability approach is mistaken. The Wittgensteinian would no doubt argue that unthinkability, as I am using it, is a meaningless concept, and that I have not succeeded in making it intelligible by my remarks in Section 7.2. But the force of his claim would depend on the reasons he advances in support of it. In Chapter 7 I anticipated several possible objections to the unthinkability approach. It may be that my defense against those objections is weak and open to further attack. But without knowing what the further attack might be, I cannot discuss this possibility any further. Another possibility is that there are important objections which I neglected to take up at all. I doubt that a Wittgensteinian would pursue this line of attack, but I shall discuss it briefly anyway.

One objection which I did not take up explicitly is that there are necessary falsehoods with respect to which the thinkability test is simply not applicable. For example, any arithmetical falsehood would serve to illustrate this point, such as the following:

(93) $2 + 2 \neq 4$.
(94) 22 is divisible by 3.

The thinkability test seems inappropriate with respect to these sentences, because one cannot readily form mental images of the things referred to in them.

I have two replies to this objection. First of all, it is not an objection to the central thesis of the book (namely, thesis (II)), but rather, to the extension of that thesis to non-type-crossings (such as arithmetical falsehoods). As far as the book is con-

cerned, I could simply give up the attempt to apply the thinkability test to non-type-crossings and confine the test to the area of
type crossings, an area in which it *is* clearly applicable.

However, quite apart from the position put forward in the
present book, I *do* want to maintain that *all* necessary falsehoods
(including arithmetical falsehoods) designate unthinkable propositions. My main reply, then, to the objection presented is that
sentences such as (93) and (94) do designate unthinkable propositions. One way this reply may be supported is by appeal to the
following two principles:

(E) Any proposition which entails an unthinkable proposition is
   itself unthinkable.
(F) All propositions of the form "p and not-p" are unthinkable.

It may be argued that the propositions designated by (93) and
(94) entail self-contradictions and, therefore, by virtue of principles (E) and (F), are to be regarded as unthinkable. There are
also other ways to support the reply given, but we need not go into these.

This objection which pertains to the application of the thinkability test is very basic and important. I suspect that, ultimately,
the only way to satisfactorily answer it will be to develop a
theory of thinkability consisting of an entire *system* of principles
similar to (E) and (F). But, needless to say, such an enterprise
goes far beyond the scope of the present book, and so I shall
here have to leave the matter unresolved.

Another fundamental objection has to do with my appeal to
the notion of a combination of concepts. The argument may be
put this way:

(1) To appeal to the thinkability or unthinkability of combinations of concepts is to presuppose a Platonic view with respect to the nature of concepts.

(2) A Platonic view with respect to the nature of concepts cannot be a correct view.

(3) Therefore, any theory that appeals to the thinkability or un-

thinkability of combinations of concepts must be an incorrect theory.

I shall assume that to avoid the conclusion I must reject at least one of the premises. Actually, neither of them strikes me as clearly true. I would have to see premise (2) demonstrated in order to be convinced of its truth. And, as for premise (1), I fail to see how my use of the term 'concept' in the present book presupposes any *particular* view about the nature of concepts. It seems to me that more than one such view is compatible with what I have said about concepts.

This question about the nature of concepts is a very fundamental one. However, it is a question that applies not only to our theory of type crossings but also to any theory that employs the notion of a proposition as a combination of concepts. For example, if someone were to suggest a theory of *truth* according to which a proposition (combination of concepts) is true if and only if it . . . etc., then no matter how the theory is completed, it is open to the question pertaining to the nature of propositions and concepts. Thus, such a question is in no way peculiar to the topic of type crossings.

Here again, I must bypass the issue. I can only say that I see no reason to maintain that my use of the term 'concept' in itself presupposes (or entails) an unacceptable view with respect to the nature of concepts. Such a presupposition (or entailment) would have to be demonstrated before I could see any necessity in defending my theory of type crossings against the objection suggested. As for the Platonism-conceptualism-nominalism issue over the status of universals, I can see how I should eventually get involved in that, but the correctness of my position om type crossings does not depend on the correctness of whatever position I take on that most difficult and fundamental issue.

I acknowledge that the positive parts of this book (in which I put forward my own theory of type crossings) are not as strong as the negative parts (in which I attack other theories). I even acknowledge the possibility that there should arise some objection which I cannot answer, although I cannot now see what sort of objection that might be. In such an event, I would have to fall back on the Wittgensteinian approach and say that the question about the ultimate basis of the conceptual meaninglessness of type crossings is an unanswerable question. But, as things stand, I see no need to do this. On the contrary, the question *is* answerable, and this book constitutes an answer to it.

The reader may want to know about the possible applications of my theory of type crossings. I do not see that it needs to have any applications beyond being a correct solution to the problems about type crossings posed at the outset of the book. However, there are a few such applications anyway. The book will be of value to the following persons:

1. The epistemologist who is interested in synthetic a priori (or synthetic necessary) truth and falsehood. I hope to have shown that such truth and falsehood is possible, and is exemplified by type crossings and their negations. Furthermore, I hope to have shown that the basis of all a priori falsehood lies in the unthinkability of propositions, or at least to have provided a pattern of reasoning in terms of which such a view might be defended.

2. The theoretical linguist or philosopher of language who is interested in getting clear about the nature of sentential meaninglessness. I distinguished various important senses of the term 'meaningless': conceptual meaninglessness, type meaninglessness, and linguistic meaninglessness. It seems unlikely that anyone could go far in a study of these three sorts of meaninglessness without coming to grips with problems connected with type crossings. In this area, I hope to have provided an indispensable guide.

3. The theoretical linguist who is interested in developing a theory of grammaticality (or of degree of grammaticality). His main stumbling block will be "thing type crossings". If he wants to exclude them from the class of grammatical utterances (or the class of *completely* grammatical utterances) by means of his

theory, then he should be prepared to meet the arguments put forward in Chapter 3.

4. The logician or semanticist who is interested in constructing an artificial language. He will want to lay down formation rules governing what is to be considered a well-formed formula of the linguistic system. Possibly he would want to include type-rules among the formation rules, and if so, then he should understand the relation of those rules to natural languages, as outlined in Chapter 4. On the other hand, if he thinks that he could allow type crossings into his system as well-formed, though self-contradictory, sentences, then he should be prepared to meet the arguments against this which are put forward in Section 2.2.

5. The analytic philosopher who is interested in the concept of an implicit rule of ordinary language. It may be that the arguments used against type-rules in Chapter 4 could be extended to show that there are no implicit rules of ordinary language at all (or at least that their number is much smaller than might originally be expected). At any rate, anyone who claims that there *are* such rules should see how they fare when confronted by the arguments from missing conditions and non-linguistic response.

6. The analytic philosopher who wants to argue that, in order to be clear, philosophical discussion must be conducted in the formal mode of speech rather than the material mode of speech. I hope to have shown in Chapter 8 that although some philosophical problems call for the formal mode of speech (e.g., the problem as to the basis of the meaninglessness of "conjunction type crossings"), there are others for which it would be quite inappropriate (e.g., the problem as to the basis of the meaninglessness of "thing type crossings"). I hope to have shown, furthermore, that there are very definite criteria as to which mode of speech is appropriate in a given case.

7. The philosopher who attempts to refute others by showing that they have made "category mistakes". I hope to have demonstrated that, strictly speaking, there is no such thing as a "category mistake". It is never the case that a person knows what

a word designates but allocates it to the wrong category. On the contrary, all the alleged cases of category mistakes (e.g., someone claiming that a person's thoughts are in his brain) are actually vocabulary mistakes that happen (coincidentally) to be brought out or expressed by the utterance of a necessary falsehood (a type crossing) rather than a contingent falsehood.

8. The aesthetician or etymologist who is interested in the nature of metaphor. Actually, a metaphorical sentence, taken literally, is invariably a type crossing. Hence, by my theory, what it expresses is unthinkable. It may be that this is precisely what is entertaining or challenging about metaphor. Since it cannot be taken literally, the reader or listener is forced into reinterpreting what is presented to him.

9. The intuitionist philosopher who is interested in finding out: (a) what can be said at all about intuition, (b) how the notion of intuition can be defined, (c) how it can be shown to be objective rather than subjective. If intuition is the appeal to the thinkability test, then Chapter 7 would be of value to this philosopher.

10. The metaphysician who is interested in the "categories of being". Possibly what I have to say about the concept of the type associated with a given property (in Section 6.3) would be some relevance here, but of this I am not sure.

In spite of all these other applications, it may well be that the main value of my theory of type crossings lies in its solution to the very profound and complex problems of the nature of type crossings and the basis of their meaninglessness. What I have done is to refute the most fashionable answer to such questions (the linguistic approach) and to defend the least fashionable answer (the thinkability approach). As a result of this, I expect that the book will elicit a critical response from both philosophers and linguists. My one hope is that in addition to being critical. this response will also be enlightened.

BIBLIOGRAPHY

BOOKS AND MONOGRAPHS

Anscombe, G. E. M., *An Introduction to Wittgenstein's Tractatus* (London, Hutchinson University Library, 1959).

Carnap, Rudolph, *The Logical Syntax of Language* (New York, The Humanities Press, Inc., 1937).

Chomsky, Noam, *Syntactic Structures* (The Hague, Mouton & Co., 1957).

Hockett, C. F., *A Course in Modern Linguistics* (New York, The Macmillan Co., 1958).

Kraft, Victor, *The Vienna Circle* (New York, Philosophical Library, 1953).

Lazerowitz, Morris, *The Structure of Metaphysics* (London, Routledge and Kegan Paul, 1955).

Pap, Arthur, *Elements of Analytic Philosophy* (New York, The Macmillan Co., 1949).

Passmore, John, *Philosophical Reasoning* (New York, Charles Scribner's Sons, 1955).

Quine, W. V. O., *Mathematical Logic* (Cambridge, Harvard University Press, 1955).

Reichenbach, Hans, *Elements of Symbolic Logic* (New York, The Macmillan Co., 1947).

Russell, Bertrand, *An Inquiry into Meaning and Truth* (London, George Allen and Unwin, Ltd., 1940).

Ryle, Gilbert, *Dilemmas* (Cambridge, Cambridge University Press, 1954).

——, *Philosophical Arguments* (Oxford, Oxford University Press, 1945).

Sartre, Jean-Paul, *Being and Nothingness* (New York, Philosophical Library, 1956).

Strawson, P. F., *Introduction to Logical Theory* (London, Methuen & Co., 1952).

Urban, Wilbur M., *Language and Reality* (London, Allen and Unwin, Ltd., 1939).

Whitehead, A. N. and Bertrand Russell, *Principia Mathematica*, Volume I, second edition (Cambridge, Cambridge University Press, 1925).

ARTICLES AND PAPERS

Baker, A. J., "Category Mistakes", *Australasian Journal of Philosophy*, XXXIV (1956).

Bar-Hillel, Y., "On Syntactical Categories", *Journal of Symbolic Logic*, XV (1950).

Black, Max, "Comments on Arthur Pap's 'Types and Meaninglessness' ", American Philosophical Association, Eastern Division (December 1957).

Carnap, Rudolph, "Testability and Meaning", *Philosophy of Science*, III (1936) and IV (1937).

Chomsky, Noam, "Degrees of Grammaticalness", printed in *The Structure of Language*, ed. Jerry A. Fodor & Jerrold J. Katz (Englewood Cliffs, Prentice-Hall, Inc., 1964).

Cross, R. C., "Category Differences", *Proceedings of the Aristotelian Society*, LIX (1959).

Drange, Theodore, "The Paradox of the Non-Communicator", *Philosophical Studies*, XV (1964).

Ewing, A. C., "Meaninglessness", *Mind*, XLVI (1937).

Gandy, R. O., Review of Arthur Pap's "Types and Meaninglessness", *Journal of Symbolic Logic*, XXV (1960).

Hill, Archibald A., "Grammaticality", *Word*, XVII (1961).

Hillman, D. J., "On Grammars and Category Mistakes", *Mind*, LXXII (1963).

Katz, Jerrold J., "Semi-sentences", printed in *The Structure of Language*, ed. Jerry A. Fodor & Jerrold J. Katz (Englewood Cliffs, Prentice-Hall, Inc., 1964).

Pap, Arthur, "Types and Meaninglessness", *Mind*, LXIX (1960).

Prior, A. N., "Entities", *Australasian Journal of Philosophy*, XXXII (1954).

Ryle, Gilbert, "Categories", *Proceedings of the Aristotelian Society*, XXXIX (1938-39). Reprinted in *Logic and Language, Second Series*, ed. Antony Flew (Oxford, Basil Blackwell, 1953).

Shorter, Michael, "Meaning and Grammar", *Australasian Journal of Philosophy*, XXXIV (1956).

Smart, J. J. C., "A Note on Categories", *The British Journal for the Philosophy of Science*, IV (1953).

Sommers, Fred., "The Ordinary Language Tree", *Mind*, LXVIII (1959).

Ziff, Paul, "About Grammaticalness", *Mind*, LXXIII (1964).

AUTHOR INDEX

TERMINOLOGICAL INDEX

JANUA LINGUARUM

STUDIA MEMORIAE NICOLAI VAN WIJK DEDICATA

Edited by Cornelis H. van Schooneveld

SERIES MINOR

22. E. F. HADEN, M. S. HAN and Y. W. HAN: A Resonance Theory for Linguistics. 1962. 51 pp.   Gld. 7.—

23. SAMUEL R. LEVIN: Linguistic Structures in Poetry. Second printing 1964. 64 pp.   Gld. 8.—

24. ALPHONSE JUILLAND and JAMES MACRIS: The English Verb System. 1962. 81 pp.   Gld. 8.—

25. IVAN FONÁGY: Die Metaphern in der Phonetik. Ein Beitrag zur Entwicklungsgeschichte des wissenschaftlichen Denkens. 1963. 132 pp., 5 figs.   Gld. 14.—

26. H. MOL: Fundamentals of Phonetics. I: The Organ of Hearing. 1963. 70 pp., 28 figs.   Gld. 9.—

27. LÁSZLÓ ANTAL: Questions of Meaning. 1963. 95 pp.   Gld. 10.—

29. PUNYA SLOKA RAY: Language Standardization. Studies in Prescriptive Linguistics. 1963. 159 pp.   Gld. 16.—

30. PAUL L. GARVIN: On Linguistic Method. Selected Papers. 1964. 158 pp.   Gld. 14.—

31. LÁSZLÓ ANTAL: Content, Meaning, and Understanding. 1964. 63 pp.   Gld. 8.—

32. GEORGES MOUNIN: La Machine à Traduire. Histoire des problèmes linguistiques. 1964. 209 pp.   Gld. 22.—

33. ROBERT E. LONGACRE: Grammar Discovery Procedure. A Field Manual. 1964. 162 pp.   Gld. 9.—

34. WILLIAM S. COOPER: Set Theory and Syntactic Description. 1964. 52 pp.   Gld. 8.—

35. LUIS J. PRIETO: Principes de noologie. Fondements de la théorie fonctionnelle du signifié. Préface d'André Martinet. 1964. 130 pp., 36 figs.   Gld. 18.—

36. SEYMOUR CHATMAN: A Theory of Meter. 1965. 229 pp., many graphs, 2 plates.   Gld. 21.—

37. WAYNE TOSH: Syntactic Translation. 1965. 162 pp., 58 figs.,
                                    Gld. 21.—

38. NOAM CHOMSKY: Current Issues in Linguistic Theory. 1964. 119 pp.   Gld. 10.—

39. D. CRYSTAL and R. QUIRK: Systems of Prosodic and Paralinguistic Features in English. 1964. 94 pp., 16 plates.   Gld. 12.—

MOUTON & CO · PUBLISHERS · THE HAGUE